GOSPEL FROM THE CITY

BRITISH LIBERATION THEOLOGY
Edited by Chris Rowland and John Vincent

1. LIBERATION THEOLOGY UK

2. GOSPEL FROM THE CITY

In Preparation

3. LIBERATION SPIRITUALITY

4. BIBLE AND LIBERATION

Further volumes under consideration.

British Liberation Theology is published under the auspices of the British Liberation Theology Project, the Institute for British Liberation Theology of the Urban Theology Unit and the Las Casas Network. The Management Group of the British Liberation Theology Project is: Rev Inderjit Bhogal, Dr Andrew Bradstock, Bishop Laurie Green, Prof. Christopher Rowland, Ms Bridget Rees, Mr Mike Simpson, Dr John Vincent and Sister Margaret Walsh. Bridget Rees and John Vincent are Joint Co-ordinators of the Institute.

The annual volumes of British Liberation Theology are available on subscription or as single books. Single copies may be obtained price £7.50, p&p 50p. A subscription to all three of the first volumes (1,2 and 3) can be obtained price £20 inc. p&p. Normal discounts (35%) are available to booksellers. Quantities of 20 or over are available to other organisations at a special discount (25%) Cheques to URBAN THEOLOGY UNIT.

Address all enquiries to: URBAN THEOLOGY UNIT, 210 Abbeyfield Road, Sheffield, S4 7AZ.

GOSPEL FROM THE CITY

**Edited by
CHRIS ROWLAND
and
JOHN VINCENT**

**Sheffield
URBAN THEOLOGY UNIT**

(c) Copyright Urban Theology Unit 1997
First published 1997

ISBN: 0 907490 07 7

Urban Theology Unit is Registered Charity No. 505334

URBAN THEOLOGY UNIT
210 Abbeyfield Road
Sheffield
S4 7AZ

Typeset by Anne Lewis and Kathy Bhogal at the Urban Theology Unit.

Printed by Tartan Press, Attercliffe, Sheffield

CONTENTS

7

EDITORIAL NOTE

BRITISH LIBERATION THEOLOGY is the overall title for a series of Bi-annual Volumes, designed to bring together new writing in the UK, using the methods of Liberation Theology, and recording the practice and spirituality of people involved in liberation struggles in Britain.

LIBERATION THEOLOGY UK was the first volume, intended to set the scene for a British Liberation Theology within the wider context of world-wide liberation theologies, and to indicate some of the ways in which liberation theology has worked and is working in contemporary thinking and discipleship. The level of the chapters in the volume was intentionally academic and pastoral. It shows how British theologies of liberation both see themselves alongside those of other continents, and also pursue distinctive indigenous agendas.

The two following volumes begin at the other end - the levels specifically of pastoral and popular practice. This second volume, GOSPEL FROM THE CITY, contains the stories, the theology and the spirituality of several contemporary disciples and groups, who see themselves as putting into practice or being motivated by liberation theology. They are stories of the practice of liberation in the urban scene today. The third volume, LIBERATION SPIRITUALITY, records some practice and reflection in terms of the lifestyle, discipleship, and prayer which are found among liberation-style practitioners.

The work of specific "branches" of liberation theology goes on primarily elsewhere - Feminist Theology, Black Theology, Regional Theologies, Lesbian and Gay Theologies, Womanist Theology. We have no wish to presume to "take over" the whole scene, though we do hope to have chapters or possibly volumes which reflect these growing and productive areas in which liberation theology proceeds from the stand-point of particular groups. Indeed, it might be that our effort will encourage them also into wider publication. Of course, that would certainly not be the case for Feminist Theology, which has already created highly significant developments, and which has certainly blazed the trail both for a more general liberation theology, and also for liberation theologies from the stand-points of the women and men oppressed in other ways.

We hope at various times to include theological discussions concerning the wider theological debates in Britain, and the legitimacy or appropriateness of British liberation theologies, especially taking into account the use made of liberation theology perspectives in other contemporary British theologians. But there has been a tendency to discuss such matters in an abstract fashion - witness the endless papers, articles and chapters on the theme "What is the relevance of liberation theology to British Christians/Churches/Theology?" It may be a useful change to postpone such theoretical questions for a few years, and let some of those who want to work this way get on and see what they can produce.

We would like to invite readers to offer contributions (4,000-6,000 words). After urban liberation theology and liberation spirituality, later volumes will cover biblical theology, political theology, and practical issues in personal, community, political and public life, from liberation theology viewpoints. Please address enquiries to either of us:

CHRIS ROWLAND
Queen's College, Oxford, OX1 4AW

JOHN VINCENT
Urban Theology Unit, Sheffield, S4 7AZ

October 1997

INTRODUCTION

As we observe in the Editorial Note, this volume begins in "the stories, the theology and the spirituality of several contemporary disciples and groups, who see themselves as putting into practice or being motivated by liberation theology." It is, consequently, mainly a volume of stories, of experiences, of happenings, and of theologically-inspired insights or discernments into them.

Liberation theologians call theology "the second act". I have often said, "Better, the forty-second act". But the point is that theologising is an ancillary, supportive, confirming, exposing or explicating activity, designed as an adjunct to something else, as its accompaniment, its comment, or its significance-discerning. The first act is practice, action, activity, happenings, political deeds, community deeds, personal deeds, each and all of which relate somehow to the central Gospel dynamic of the Kingdom presence, of liberation for the oppressed, of people empowerment, of disciple emboldment, and of political/social/economic confrontation and change.

What is striking, it seems to me, in the present volume is that the practice and the theology are indistinguishable, or at least go hand in hand, or at times follow each other, or at other times, provide language for each other. Nowhere do the writers suddenly stop and say, "Now I must do some theological refection". Rather, the theology is within the stories and the actions. And the stories and the actions get told here because they were already liberation-theology-style Gospel stories - that is, theologically influenced pieces of story and action.

Thus, Jane Grinonneau does not know whether she begins with herself and her people with the street kids of Allens Cross, or the Jesus of the Gospels with the streetkids of Galilee. Diane Butler describes the deprived life of her estate and the life Jesus chose for himself, then creates for herself a life coherent with both, and finally asks, "Is this not what it is all about?" Jan Royan tells a story of her own "Option for the Poor", and implicitly demands that we accord the same hearing and status for the urban poor in Britain as we do for those in Nicaragua - and, of course, ends up herself in a different place. Linda Granville puts herself before us as one of those alongside whom we are to minister, and says, Can you not see some marks of Jesus here also? Moby Farrands has an ear to the Jesus of the Gospel working among the people of his time, and finds the same things happening on the streets of Radford.

Margaret Walsh pursues her Heath Town incarnation, and discovers elements of the archetypal Jesus community in the resulting fellowship of carers and cared for in their post-church (but new Christian?) life together with the poor. Inderjit Bhogal walks out onto the streets of Pitsmoor and finds the realities far more coherent with a Jesus of many faiths than with the doctrinal Christ of orthodoxy. Duncan Wilson proclaims specific aspects of the New Testament versions of Base Christian Communities, alive and well in the despised, small, street-corner congregations of the left-behind in the inner city.

Theology is not so much the "second act", and practice the "first act" - as that theology and practice are two steps, one following the other, as one walks along. It becomes explicit in the last three pieces, perhaps more consciously analytical and theological than the others.

Laurie Green and I try more specifically to relate all this to the Gospel of Jesus. Laurie retells the classic tale of Jesus and his contemporaries, in terms of the Underclass, and derives from it striking insights into some contemporary attitudes and policies. I ask whether it does not all amount to a new Hearing for the Gospel, inasmuch as a new group of people, the urban disciples of the late 20th century, suddenly begin to hear the Galilean tales as their own tales, and find the responses of others around them remarkably like the responses of Jesus' critics. Says Chris Rowland, it is indeed a bit of a problem to the theologian and the academy to find the stories and sagas and theologies that theologians study in the academy, actually being picked up and being used, not just being heard, by contemporary non-academics. A new theology - and a new academy - are surely the next steps. UTU was a first venture in those directions. What now?

Our Methodist Report on The Cities calls for "an expanding and inclusive theology of and for the City, which arises out of the discipleship of its members." (1) Here is a start.

JOHN VINCENT

(1) The Cities: A Methodist Report (NCH Action for Children: 1997)
     Recommendation 1.3, p 222

Jane Grinonneau

CITY KIDS AS SIGNS OF THE KINGDOM

1. Home Ground and Harsh Reality

Allens Cross is a 1930's council development showing all the signs of urban deprivation. It forms a clearly defined physical area bordered on all four sides by busy roads including the Bristol Road.

The Census in 1991 shows Allens Cross has a population of 8,130 which includes 2,259, (25%) children under 15 years of age (1). There are 271 lone parent households (an increase of 129.7% in ten years). The survey also identified that 15% of the total population of Birmingham is under 10 years of age, and 19% in Allens Cross. The Conservative Government policy of the right-to-buy has meant that many houses on the estate have been purchased. From a total of 3,113 dwellings 1,285 are owner-occupied; 1,548 rented from local authority and the remainder are managed by the Housing Association or are privately rented. Council property is frequently of poor quality, damp and with old wiring.

Staff from the local branch of Social Services admit excessive demands on their time. Their work has become more risk assessment than supportive of struggling families. One Team Leader has recently begun a local branch of Home Start. This is a national charitable organisation designed to bring alongside families in difficulties, experienced but non-professional people to support and befriend them. Middlemore Family Centre, bordering the estate, is a Birmingham Charity established in 1872. It is part funded by and works closely with the Social Services Department. Its concern has

Jane Grinonneau was Associate Minister at Northfield Baptist Church, Birmingham, 1991-96. In September 1996 she became minister at the Furnival public house church in the Sheffield Inner City Ecumenical Mission, and a part-time tutor at UTU.

been developing good parent/child relationships and a broad range of skills. The majority of their user group are drawn from Allens Cross and the two adjacent estates. Criminal activity committed by those under 10 years of age is high and recorded juvenile crime of 11 - 18 is also high. An interview with the local bobby revealed that this area of Northfield is regarded as the worst beat for police in the area. Criminal activity 'has reached an unmanageable level' (2).

In 1986, the estate lost its secondary school, in a major secondary education reorganisation. There were 800 pupils on the roll at the time. Secondary school children now have to bus out to more distant education provision. This closure resulted in the loss of a significant focus for the estate. The two local schools taking the majority of the children 5 -11 years, from the estate, record eligibility for free school meals as 85% and 56%, indicating high levels of low income families in the area. Food distribution is undertaken by several local agencies for families who have run out of money for food. The furniture project run by the churches has grown to be the second largest in Birmingham, such is the demand. The Northfield branch of the Citizens Advice Bureau says that debt can be seen as the root of most problems (3).

There are no safe acceptable play areas within the estate. Play activities or opportunities are limited to uniformed church-based activities and two clubs run by the Community Worker which are for 5 - 11 years olds and have a capacity of only 30 places. The children often play 'chicken' and other games in the road. Older youths hang about in groups and drift between two pubs situated on the borders of the estate. The children are often the topic of conversation among the adults on street corners and in shops (and in church). 'Terrible how they behave'. Jacob's dream at Bethel is a powerful reminder that God is in every place, although we, like Jacob need to wake up to the fact!

'He is in this place and I did not know it' (Gen. 28:16).

Allens Cross, with all its contrasts and conflicts, with some people living in hope and others oppressed to the point of non-participation in any aspect of community life, has all the potential of a place open to heaven, because God is present. The signs of God's presence are visible in the gentle goodness of many who live here and those who stand with them interpreting, in their own language, the undiscovered nature of God. In the 1950s and 1960s a number of the leaders and active members of the young people's work of the adjacent Northfield Baptist Church, where I work, lived on Allens Cross. In addition, during this period three members of the church who came from Allens Cross were ordained.

My ground too!

I was called to Northfield, my first pastorate, in 1991. My background has been in nursing, adult education and counselling. At 42 years old, it was through my experience of divorce and serious heart disease that I discovered the reality of God and became compelled by 'the love of Christ' to reach others with the radical Good News. I had felt a strong if inexplicable 'feel' for Northfield at my very first visit and knew once appointed, that I must live on Allens Cross. 'The Little Manse' as it came to be known, in contrast to The Manse the 'other' side of the Bristol Road, where traditionally Baptist Ministers have lived, is an end of terrace Council house. From the outside there is little to commend it yet it has become central to ministry among discouraged and disaffected people, the abused, homeless and hungry. The veranda at the back of the kitchen, until recently, has been a blanket, clothing and general household store providing a ready supply of essentials. When I first moved in , in 1991, the house quickly became a place for kids to come. Every Monday afternoon the lounge was full of children, drinking orange juice, eating biscuits, and creating things! As the months passed, it was obvious 'we' would have to move to a bigger venue.

2. Seeing and Responding

Northfield Baptist Church was founded in 1912 with 22 members. It is situated in the centre of Northfield adjacent to the A38 Bristol Road, on the edge of Allens Cross estate, but it has only been on this site since 1937. In 1935, the newly inducted minister set the re-location of the church as a condition of his acceptance of the call to the pastorate. The building was on the Banbury Road, but he had a vision for the church in the heart of the growth area, on the edge of Allens Cross estate. There were about 350 children attending Sunday school on Allens Cross! The current site of the church was then positioned behind some old shops, of which a few, like the butcher's, still remain. It was purchased in February 1936 from a farmer in the village. The plan for Northfield was to demolish the old shops and widen the road leaving the Church with a wide frontage site. The Church was built in 1937, but after the war the road widening was shelved and eventually abandoned. In the 1960s planning permission was given to rebuild shops in front of the Church, against church protests! A small corner of the frontage land was sold at a greatly inflated price to enable the corner shop to be roughly rectangular. This income helped in a small way toward the cost of the church re-development in 1972.

Since the 1970s the church building had been subject to increasing vandalism to the extent that metal mesh was fitted to the windows to prevent the weekly breaking of windows. The through-way for pedestrians between the Bristol Road in the front and the Allens Cross behind the church, passing as it did over a disused, land-locked area, made the church vulnerable to vandalism. After much discussion about the problem there appeared a visionary solution. It was agreed with the City to develop this land-locked area. In partnership with Baptist Housing (now English Churches Housing Association) and the Social Services a sheltered housing complex for the elderly, Ash Grove, was built and opened in 1986. This created an impenetrable barrier between the estate and the church. The vandalism stopped and so did much of the contact which had been established with the people of Allens Cross. However, engagement with the neighbourhood continued through the Girls and Boys Brigades; through the Luncheon Club which was established 21 years ago catering for 80 people every Wednesday, through points of fellowship in several Clubs; and through Friday Lunch Break, based at the Baptist Church because of its central location, but an ecumenical activity, serving light lunches to, on average, 30-50 shoppers between 12-1.30pm.

It was as more young people came into the Brigades that awareness grew of the many complex social problems existing just outside the door of the church. Issues concerning abuse, debt, broken relationships and drug dependency became familiar challenges to those working alongside the young people. How could the church respond to these cries of distress? After a formal review of the life of the church conducted in 1989-90 it was decided by the membership to call a second minister to help develop the contacts between the church and the neighbourhood. Thus, I appeared on the scene.

Fun Club

Kids Clubs Network is a registered charity promoting creative play provision. This facility is especially important in areas of deprivation where play opportunities are often scarce. It seems like a major undertaking to gather the children from the estate onto church premises but .... The Out of School Development Officer for the City was approached regarding a substantial grant to underwrite the scheme. We knew that with so many families on income support, sessional payments would have to be minimal or

15

we would exclude the very children we wanted to reach most. Staffing, equipment, compliance with employment and Social Services legislation did not deter us! Funding was granted, church agreement obtained, and Fun Club came into being. The children aged 5 - 11 years came slowly at first but it was not long before the scheme was running to capacity. Every day in term time, between the hours of 3pm and 6pm the church is 'taken-over' by the children and the team of staff. In the beginning it was hard, the behaviour of many children was a challenge and several people in the church found their language offensive and their indiscipline hard to tolerate. Central to every session was a hot two-course meal shared together at the table. Several children found this a novel experience, being unfamiliar with the skills needed to use a knife and fork, or to sit still and eat with others. Food flew sometimes, cabbage stuck to carpets and chairs, peas rolled into unimaginable places as if to draw attention to the enormous struggle of keeping order. But it worked. Gradually over months the children's behaviour became less aggressive and opportunity for creative and co-operative play increased. Parents' trust increased too, and slowly interest in the work increased to the point of getting up a petition to the City to secure further funding. But other, unexpected things happened. Among the Members of the Church there was a new openness; a deeper warmth, and a readiness to share. What was happening to explain this?

3. A Biblical Tale

Birmingham is a place of stark contrasts and extremes. The city boasts the Symphony Hall, exhibition centres, a network of canal-side restaurants, all beautiful but expensive. Areas of lavish development stand adjacent to areas of deprivation. This pattern is continued out in the urban areas and is certainly visible in Northfield. The reality of life on the edge of the city is reflected in the number of 'prisons', manifest in several guises. Injustice, inequality, fear, hopelessness create a captivity no less effective than that made of bricks and mortar.

What's new? Oppression and injustice have been the stuff of every generation. The poor are denied justice, there is corruption by those with power. Corrupt men of law (Ps. 94:20), corrupt rulers (Ecc. 5:5-17), corrupt employers (Jer. 22:13; Mt. 20:1f), corrupt people of God (Is. 58:1-7; Amos 5:10ff). But, with the coming of Jesus, Mark tells us, the Kingdom of God is at hand, an era of justice and healing, reconciliation and wholeness (Mk. 1:15). The entry qualification is childlikeness (Mt. 18:1-3). Judgement comes to those who cause the little ones to lose faith (Mt. 18:6). What determines whether we experience grace or judgement depends upon the response made to the little ones, those considered by the world to be of no account - the hungry, cold and imprisoned (Mt. 25:31-46).

My MMin Site-Team at Northfield Baptist Church had studied 'biblical perspectives', believing that such exploration would cast light on the people of Allens Cross. The light indeed fell upon Allens Cross, but a penetrating light fell also upon 'us' the Church. In our attempts to get at what the bible was saying, the bible somehow got at us! Having been with the people around Jesus we caught a glimpse of how we looked as the people of Jesus around Allens Cross. This new perception was liberating and challenging. What does it mean to be the people of God? What did Jesus mean when he said only children can enter the Kingdom? And, confronted with oppressive forces, what must the church do to enable the Kingdom of God 'to be earthed' (Matt 6:10)?

If we are genuine about our undertaking to examine ourselves as God's community we need to dispose of any cherished 'dream' of ourselves. Bonhoffer writes:

Innumerable times a whole Christian community has broken down because it had sprung from a dream wish. God's grace speedily shatters such dreams ... He who loves his dream of a community more than the Christian community itself becomes a destroyer of the latter. (4)

It seemed to us, as we brought the bible into our situation, that some unseen power had been unleashed. Like the filling in a sandwich, it linked Church with God and Allens Cross. Had we previously kept them apart? Now a new energy was released which was beyond our control and which, having been let out, swirled around, exposing all manner of perceptions and making new and exciting connections. God's project (5) had always been about justice and wholeness, and that precluded any partiality of any kind. It was a dangerous dream for the Church to believe that it was detached from neighbourhood and world. Rather, its energising from God was dependent on its very connections with God and the world. God's theocratic rule would bring the light into the darkness of the world (6).

The dynamic power of the Kingdom operates in a decisive way and demands decision. It demands an alternative lifestyle of solidarity in marked contrast to self-interest. It demands solidarity with the weak. Does that mean that our way to the Kingdom is through solidarity with the little ones around us? They are voiceless and powerless to achieve change. They may not be orphaned, although they may never see their fathers (7). They may not sleep on the streets as children do in the Third World, but too many are abused and disadvantaged by patterns of parenting (8) and the effects of poverty and urban living (9). Shall we preach the Kingdom and set the captives free?

Is setting the captives free even the means to our own freedom?

A Surprising Picnic

One day, Jesus met people on their journey and surprised them with an unforgettable lesson. The story is in John 6.1-12. The picture given to us is of a crowd moving towards Jerusalem for the Passover Festival, marking Israel's delivery from slavery in Egypt. Jesus did not wait to greet them as they arrived at the temple but went out to them. Only the men are counted in the assessment of the crowd, for only they are considered worthy of reckoning, but there were women and children too. Hungry people and anxious disciples look to Jesus. He receives nothing from the powerful Jewish leaders or teachers, but from the hands of a child Jesus receives loaves and fish - all the child had to give. This hints at a Johannine last supper and offers us too, the symbolism of the tribes of Israel gathered together. As one in the crowd - what did we see? A miracle yes, but the miracle was not so much in the 'manufacture' of what was not there by some super-natural force but the releasing to be shared freely in community of what before was kept hidden for individual benefit.

A child, not even worthy of inclusion in the statistic, becomes the agent of liberation for the educated and powerful. The despised child, representing all those deemed as of no account, held in his hands the means through which Christ worked. In this act of radical sharing, everyone had more than enough. 'When they had eaten their fill' (Jn. 6:12), there was still food left over (Jn. 6:13). The weak liberate the strong. Jesus shows people, powerful, well versed in the Law and steeped in tradition, a new passover bringing the liberation of the world (Jn. 3:16) quite irrespective of religion or place, quality or qualification (Jn. 4:21,23).

So the weak become of blessing for the strong. This insight sent us back to reflect again on the kenosis of God and Paul's letter to the Philippians. Jesus empties himself of his equality with God in order to be incarnated with an identity which allies him with the world's little ones. His new poverty and powerlessness is to liberate the world from its perceptions of worth and power which in fact hold it in abject poverty. Just as Jesus' ultimate glorification of God rested upon the renunciation of all things (Phil. 2:8), so too for the people of God the call is to leave aside power and possessions and become allies with the weak until all experience shalom. The poor become rich, the blind see, the lame walk, those who were last become first - in God's order everything is turned upside down. Through this radical reversal of God's order of things, the kingdom of God is seen. Greatness, seen as top, powerful, master, ruler, adult, is inverted to read greatness understood as bottom, servant, slave, last, child, youngest (10). This is in fact restoration as well as reversal - a restoration to the primitive and elemental reality of human beings as little ones before a loving God who has himself become a little one in Christ.

Jesus thus shows us a powerful methodology of out-reach - going with him to meet the crowd with a readiness to both give all and receive from all, especially the 'little ones'. Bringing to him those who need the touch of the kingdom and being prepared to be surprised by the new thing he goes on doing! As we help the people of Allens Cross so we see more clearly the kingdom at hand and find our own blessing.

So, planning alongside theologising, we finally came to putting something into practice - The Project.

4. The Project

I leave aside the details of the Project of Play and Child Development which we carried out. I concentrate on the people who ran it and the little people who came to it.

The Project's People

Dawn and I stood in the large, empty hall of the church, which was to be the venue for the Project. In the preceding months, we had spent hours discussing the possibilities of doing something for the kids on the street. Now the dream was emerging from the mists of that hope - soon the kids would be coming to the playscheme, but we wondered would they come? Formal interview for the post of Project Leader seemed unnecessary in view of the months of preparatory debate, in which we had established a framework and a philosophy for the play-scheme. It had to be more than just a place to contain the kids for three hours a day. It had to be a place where they and their parents experienced, however inadequately, the love of

Jesus. The issue of Dawn's appointment was discussed with the diaconate, who were unanimous in their consent.

Dawn is in her early thirties, mother of three children under 9 years. She has been a Member of the Church for many years and has contributed greatly to a wide range of children's and young people's activities. She is employed part-time, teaching children with special needs, at her neighbourhood infant and primary school. Dawn has many gifts, relates warmly to children and has an ability to make something beautiful out of nothing!

June has children, but hers are grown and away from home. She was appointed as assistant play-care worker, working alongside Dawn. Being older, she has the feel of 'granny' but the spirit and energy of a play-mate. June undertakes much of the food purchasing and monitors the preparation of food too. June is a Member of the Church.

Theresa joined the team following her successful application for the advertised post of second play-care worker. She is in her early twenties, a member of the Anglican Church and is very gifted in her work with children.

Three staff is the minimum staff-children ratio, demanded by the Social Services but additional staff are essential if the children are to receive much needed attention. A series of volunteers, committing themselves to a session a week, provided the extra staff. Community Service Volunteers have been deployed and also students from Westhill College undertaking Youth and Community Studies.

The kitchen team is led by Doreen who gives her time and talent freely to the Project. She is also studying catering at Bournville College of Further Education. Doreen, now in midlife, made the comment one day that: '....the children have stopped me being haunted by my own childhood, they have set the child within me free.' During her work with the Project, Doreen came to faith and was baptized. Several church members assist Doreen, on a voluntary and sessional basis, helping to ensure that two people are preparing meals for the 25 children and 6 staff, every session.

Diana is the Treasurer and handles the Grants and ongoing financial management of the Project. She also ensures that wages are paid promptly, salary slips received on time from the Pay-Roll Manager and that sufficient cash is available to enable the purchase of food and play resources. Diana is a deacon and provides a vital link between Project and Church. Sue is the Secretary to the Project, attending meetings and maintaining records. Sue is a church member.

The Little People

For the first week or two the Project ran at about 50% capacity - but we had anticipated this might happen. The children who did come were typical of those we desperately wanted to reach. They came from the area just behind the church, our neighbours coming to our place. They came and slowly with their vulnerability and openness, challenged our perceptions of the need to be strong and significant.

Meet Steven. He is only six years old and has already been excluded from school several times because of unmanageable behaviour. Today he comes into the hall, as always, on the look out for trouble. With his forearm flat on the puzzle table, he uses it like a radar scanner and sweeps all the puzzles to the floor. Bits of puzzle and boxes pile in a heap by the table. Mindless of the mess, he wanders off to disrupt a small group of girls playing 'shops' in one corner. As he walks around, he takes a swipe at any smaller children who happen to cross his path. At meal times things get worse as Steven will not use any cutlery, or sit on his chair - underneath it perhaps. Some days the only way he will eat anything at all is if he is fed - like a weaned baby.

It is so easy to see his behaviour in terms of disruption to our programme. Instead, what we must see, is his hurt and confusion, expressed in a 'language' we must learn to interpret. A visit to his home revealed the chaos his behaviour reflects. Here, violence is the more common means of communication in a high tension relationship between Mum and partner (not the father of Steven). There is no table at which to eat, meals are eaten sitting on the floor. The house is full of boxes and black bags, there is no order. When the atmosphere becomes explosive the children are locked in their rooms. With Social Work support, sessions at Middlemore Family Centre and supportive work with Mum, Steven's 'language' changes. He teaches us what it is like when the vulnerable become victims of the conflict of the strong. In Africa they say, the grass gets hurt when elephants fight.

.....and Matthew. Matthew is 10 years old, angry, and ready to attack. He revels in maximum disruption. His techniques include locking toilet doors - girls and boys - making his exit over the partition walls, having effectively put all toilets out of use; filling the toilet basins to capacity with paper towels; hurling himself like a human missile at any small child; making an effective weapon out of anything movable. At meal times, for Matthew, opportunity knocks. Disliked food is subject to a quick flick with thumb and second finger (reaching some amazing distances); he kicks hard, any child sat within range at the table. Yet, one day he responded to a request for help to rearrange the food in the emergency food store. He was brilliant in his enthusiasm and co-operation although it became apparent that he could not read the labels on the tins.

The expectation of everyone was that Matthew was always 'difficult' yet when allowed to be himself, he was not. His aggression acted like a cloak to cover all his failed attempts to fit the mould that others made for him. Have the parameters of acceptability become so visible, that those outside them are ejected to the margins of life, reduced to mere survival? Matthew's response to forces that conform, confronted us to search for conforming forces alive in the church. We found them, in the criticisms of the church members who were intolerant of the children's behaviour and unseeing of the life-trauma, of which it was a symptom.

Trusted......We had been concerned about a couple of the kids. David was 6 and his sister, Lizzy, 8. Their clothes were dirty, hair unwashed, pale faced and thin and they seldom showed any joy. One day things were more than usually strained. Mum invariably swore at the children - to them it was normal. Good-bye was often experienced by way of a stream of four-lettered words. This day, Mum had hung around uneasily and eventually accepted our invitation for a coffee and a bit of quiet in the office. She had come to breaking point and felt suicidal. She was hitting the children and her smoking consumed the majority of the limited income which meant the children were often hungry. The strain of poverty and the effects of poor and damp housing left its mark. Later, re-housed and with one of the children in short-term foster care, there seemed to be some hope.

Situations like this brought into sharp relief the recent research into the effects of social policy on the disadvantaged and the suffering of the little ones' as a direct consequence.

Tested.....Andrew is a bit like 'Tigger', he bounces about all over the place, very alert! He has learned, in his seven years, that survival depends on exclusive concern for number one. Stan, from the Site Team, attended the Project on a regular basis for a few weeks, playing basket-ball with the children. Each time Stan appeared, Andrew looked at him, called him Grandad and asked: 'You gonna play?' Stan emphasised the need to pass the ball among the group and demonstrated this at every opportunity so all the players could try to score. When Andrew had the ball, he would not pass it to the other players but hung onto it for as long as possible. Weeks passed and Stan's time at the Project ended, but later, he made an unscheduled visit and met with Andrew again. Andrew's question was: 'Hi Grandad, you gonna play - we'll pass the ball?' Stan was non-threatening and so co-operation became a possibility - after all it was more fun that way!

Some children did come from stable homes where love and acceptance were the norm. Some found the conduct of others intimidating to the point that they no longer attended. It would have been easy to stop the troublesome children from coming, but that was not an option for us. Despite having to survive against the odds, these children had retained their true nature, although many had learned how to protect it from the onslaught of further pain. Once released from the havoc and expectations of the adult world, they did become more like children, spontaneous, creative, fun-loving and less aggressive.

And us? For the first few months of the Project, the staff met with considerable antagonism. The children's noise, 'bad' language, lack of discipline, the damaged furniture, the writing on the walls and high levels of aggressive behaviour, provided plenty of ammunition for those against the scheme. But slowly, as more church members actually met the children through their commitment to working a session, or more casual contact, things changed.

Liberation is a process which takes time. We had to first see and hear ourselves through the perceptions of the children. 'Out of the mouths of babes and infants' (Ps. 8:2). Their childlikeness mirrored to us what we should be, yet were not.

So, back we went to the Jesus stuff!

5. Children Only!

The Kingdom is promised to all who are ready to receive it, but it must be received 'like a child' (Mk. 10:15). Between the exposition on entry to the kingdom given by Jesus to the rich young man and his statement that entry into the kingdom is impossible for humans (Mk. 10:27), Jesus says how hard it is to enter the kingdom of God (Mk. 10:24). Paul uses the term 'child' somewhat disparagingly when writing to the churches (1Cor. 13:11;

14:20; Gal. 4. 1-3; Eph. 4:14). However when the disciples are preoccupied with their debate about power and prestige in the kingdom (Mt. 18:1), Jesus uses both the presence (Mt. 18:2) and the stature (Mt. 18:3, Lk. 18:17) of a child, to illustrate the necessary state for entry into the kingdom. There is nothing ambivalent about it. Unless there is both turning to and changing into childlikeness there is no entry into the kingdom. As if to leave no room for doubt, Jesus adds 'whoever shares the humility of the child will become the greatest in the kingdom of heaven' (Mt. 18:4).

There are two possible meanings to 'receiving the kingdom as a child'. It could mean, 'receive the kingdom as a child receives things', or 'receive the kingdom as you would receive a child'. In Disciple and Lord, J. J. Vincent indicates the implications of both interpretations. If it means 'receive the kingdom as a child receives':

> The child, then is held up as a living embodiment of what the disciple must be. To receive the kingdom is to be as a child, and receive a gift with joy and surprise, as a child does (11).

If it means 'receive the kingdom as you receive a child':

> The kingdom is to be received as one receives a child. Disciples are to welcome the kingdom, as Jesus welcomes the child (Mk. 9:36) (12)

Entry Criteria

What is unique to the condition of this childlikeness that it alone acts as key to the kingdom? The mind may conjure the image of the choir-boy on the Christmas card or the Artful Dodger in Oliver. Most people with experience of children would probably say children move between both extremes. But it is not quirks of character that open the door to the kingdom but states of being in relation to God.

1. Not by learning. The child is full of potential, with room for growth, in body mind and spirit. The child readily owns its need for growth. Being 'grown up' is something to aim for although as yet it is unachieved. Jesus does not say 'Grow up' to the children, but he does say to the adults 'Grow down'. To those perceiving themselves mature and well-informed this must have been hard to hear. Jesus confronts the respected and learned men, scrupulous in their observance of the Torah, with the truth that it is not by fulness of understanding nor observance of the Law, that entry into the kingdom is gained. The children with little understanding or knowledge are

24

already there! The young and vulnerable 'have it' over the wise and prudent (13). The well-educated may in fact have their minds closed to new understanding, making them fixed in belief and resistant to new possibilities and further growth. Children however are spontaneous, curious and hungry for new things.

2. Not by status. The child is powerless and unable alone to overcome the difficulties others place in its path (14). Yet into this very powerlessness Jesus calls his disciples (Mt. 18:2). From this position of powerlessness, Jesus takes the weak and places them at his side (Lk. 9:47). The disciples by their attitude and behaviour toward the children demonstrate the attitude of society as a whole - that children yet have to become of worth. They are of worth only when they are big enough to adopt the qualities, behaviours and values set before them by adults. The humility of the child, however, is found in the recognition of apparent worthlessness as reflected in the responses of those around them! The disciples were caught up in their concern for hierarchy and status (15). Peter and James and John all claim positions of power (Mk. 10:35) - or their mother asks for them (Mt. 20:20-1). Kraybill comments on Mk. 9:37:

> The bossing mentality is accompanied by the social comparison process which ranks people from greatest to least. Jesus rebuked this clamouring for status and power by taking a child in his arms. (16)

Later, the disciples were filtering out the unimportant visitors to Jesus, pushing to one side mothers and children who wanted blessing (Mk. 10:13-14). Children were of no account and women little more. But here they were getting in the way of Jesus' important mission. Jesus said 'Let the children come', and he took the child and blessed it saying 'The kingdom of God belongs to children' (Mk. 10:15). True humility is having an accurate assessment of worth. Separate from Christ, no one can gain access to the kingdom. Children are under no illusion of worthiness, and therefore provide the example of a true assessment of the human situation in relation to God.

3. Not by wealth. Children have few possessions. Then, as now, they are unlikely to have access to much money. The difference now is that advertising deceives the child into the belief that possessions themselves are indicators of the worth of those who own them. Many possessions equals much worth - few possessions equals worth-lessness. The value of life becomes welded to the value of possessions. The rich man treasured his possessions and could not bear to part with them despite the fact that they

obstructed his access into the kingdom (17). Jesus says, 'Where your treasure is, there is your heart' (Mk. 6:21). For Jesus there was nowhere even to lay his head (Mt. 8:20). Worldly treasure, far from being an asset, is an obstruction to kingdom entry, as it acts as a distraction from the obedience to Christ which discipleship demands (Mk. 9: 42-48).

4. Not by power. The child is usually in a relationship of dependency through which physical, emotional and spiritual needs are met. The child does not question this relationship, but openly receives from the parent all that the parent seeks to give. In this security, the child can be spontaneous, curious, exploring the world around and finding joy in sharing these things with the 'parent'. The child thus signals for all that in the realisation of dependency upon the Father, in the recognition of powerlessness, seeking after the kingdom of God and not investing in the world (Mt. 6: 33), is the way to the kingdom of God.

5. Not with hands full. The kingdom of God is promised to anyone who will receive it like a child (Mt. 10: 15). The child which Jesus reached out to allowed himself to be lifted from his own ground where he had been standing and raised up to be with Christ. This may appear to be pushing the text hard, but in reality it was what happened. The child surrendered to the open hands of Christ. Of course, a child cannot resist the greater strength of an adult and will either struggle in an attempt to get free, or surrender to the embrace. Most children anticipating a welcome embrace by an adult, will stretch out their arms to assist being gathered up. Is this surrender to the kingdom, as the child surrendered to Jesus, an important aspect of entry into the kingdom?

What of the openness of the hands of the child? Observe a child receiving a gift. Seldom is it done with timidity. Rather, the parcel is grabbed and paper torn from the package as if life itself depended upon it! No reticence but impatient to take all! Is this the way to receive the gift of the kingdom?

Of course, to take anything fully into our hands necessitates the hands being empty of other things. Jesus calls his disciples to give up what they had held and valued, because in their losing everything, they would gain so much more (Mk. 10:21, 29-30). But as nothing, with nothing.....so that everything God would give may be received.

In the child we can see the image that God requires for the entry of anyone and everyone, into the kingdom. Entry is open to all who recognise their powerlessness to enter without Jesus (Mk. 10: 27). Entry is open to those who are both poor and small in the world's stature ratings; to those who allow Christ to take them and lift them to himself; to those who are open unashamedly to receive from and own their Lord (18).

6. The Child as Agent of the Kingdom

(1) To the Church

In Mark, the whole debate about childlikeness is within the context of discipleship. The disciples with Jesus have given up much to follow their Lord (Mk. 10:28). However they do not seem to have understood the advantage this inevitably brings to them, ie entry into the kingdom.

> Mark's Jesus appears faced with this pathos, this pathetic inability of the disciples to discern even that element of the kingdom which they have already in fact grasped - renunciation. 'My children', he says to them. Can they not believe that they are his - and will share unbelievable things? Can they not enter as children, as having nothing and seeing that all they need to have is nothing? (19)

The children are visual images of the criteria of entry to the kingdom, and as such, show to the Church the essential nature of its being. The Church taking seriously the demand of Christ to live its life by the values of the kingdom will take equally seriously the kingdom entry criteria, and so be childlike. The Church.....

> .....would be considered exasperating and irresponsible by some and refreshing by others. It might often be in trouble with someone but it would consider it more important to be right with God. It would be light of heart and tenacious of purpose, a community of rejoicing and a community of resistance. It would be generous to people beyond its own immediate circle. (20)

The Church as a child recognises its dependence on God and lives trusting God through faith. It can never be a place of the kingdom **and** a place of oppressive, conforming forces. It has no choice but to be powerless, yet, in the power of the kingdom, challenges the ways of the world, when they oppose the kingdom way. Jesus, filled with the Spirit of the kingdom, went into the place of emptiness, and was tempted to be re-filled from the world (21). His resistance to power, possessions and status, showed us, who would be disciples, what must be our way too. A discipleship community, seeing itself as living by childlikeness, adopts alternative methods and experiences, and becomes involved in some radically alternative happenings.

The children showed the Church what it means to be out-of-control, out-of-power, to be without status. It was as if they showed to us the folly of our own deceptions. We proclaimed a liberating Love but lived with the compulsion to conform ourselves and others, to some perceived ideal. Their freedom set us free. As some of them struggled with the basics of using a knife and fork, somehow we were challenged about our treasured sophistication, and found it lacking. But above all, it was their acceptance of us, which released us from our need to overpower them. As they put themselves in our hands, like vulnerable but living bread and fish, somehow they became our food, and we were blessed through them.

One educated Church Member, finding the behaviour of the children in the Fun Club unacceptable, had been critical of the work. Out one day collecting for Christian Aid, she called at one of the many flats. The door opened and she was surprised to see a familiar little face (a Fun Club child) looking up at hers. With joy, the little girl rushed off and was heard to shout to her Mum, 'It's my friend at the door'! The woman was moved to tears that the child should call her friend.....and she changed. In so many ways the children showed us how to be, open, powerless and free in the truth of Christ.

(2) To the World

The Child as Agent of the Kingdom relates not only to the Church and to would-be disciples. It also is to be the 'face' and model and agent for the kingdom in the world. Jesus called disciples to make a new kind of fellowship:

Jesus called people to be sent out to preach, to communicate the good news that the kingdom of God is near, that there is a new opportunity for God's authority to work in the world, and that therefore it's worth making radical changes. Jesus called people to be sent out to stand against the powers that caused people to be less complete than the Creator intended. They were to go to challenge the powers of evil, to bring peace and healing as signs of the kingdom of God. (22)

This fellowship is to preach through its own radical life-style. By its nature, it confronts the world with the kingdom alternative to the shattered communities in neighbourhoods, nations and world. Resisting the abuse of power, the accumulation of wealth, the hunger for status, it is free in the truth and love of God, to receive with open arms the embrace of God. Its face is the face of the kingdom, warm with love yet set firm in defence of justice. Full of joy, yet with hard determination to set those held captive free.

Oppressed people, little people, are the mediation of God, as those who minister to them discover. The childlike Church, as Christ, alongside the little ones, will receive into its own new emptiness, the fulness of the kingdom.

Footnotes:

1. Office of Population Census Survey 1991, Small Area Statistics
2. Interview conducted with the local beat policewoman - Sharon Harding
3. Citizens Advice Bureau, Annual Report, 1993-94, Northfield
4. Dietrich Bonhoeffer, Life Together, London: SCM Press, 1954, p15
5. God's project had always been to re-establish justice and shalom, to restore all creation to God-centred living
6. God's theocratic rule, Exodus 20:1f; John 1:1f
7. Family Policy Studies Centre Survey of Lone Parents, cited in What On Earth Are We Doing To Our Children? Manchester: Maranatha Community, 1995
8. Family and Parenthood, York: Joseph Rowntree Foundation, 1995
9. ibid
10. D B Kraybill, The Upside-Down Kingdom, Ontario: Herald Press, 1978, pp 275-278
11. J J Vincent, Disciple and Lord, Sheffield Academy Press, 1976, p 81
12. ibid. p 81
13. Matthew 11:25; Luke 10:21-22
14. Matthew 19:13-15; Mark 10:17-31; Luke 18:18-30
15. Mark 9:33-34
16. D B Kraybill, op cit, p 273
17. Mark 10:17-31; Matthew 19:16-30; Luke 18:18-30
18. Romans 1:16
19. J J Vincent, op cit, p 80
20. Unfinished Business, Children and the Churches, The Consultative Group on Ministry among Children, London: CCBI Publications, 1995
21. Luke 4:1-13; Matthew 4:1-11; Mark 1:12-13
22. J D Davies, World on Loan, Bible Society, 1993, p 91

Diane Butler

A LIFE OF STRUGGLE AND CONFLICT

1. Ward Green Estate - Off and On

Initially, I was going to begin this paper, in true western academic style, by setting out its purpose. I decided against this and thought it was a good idea to just tell my story. After all, "to tell the story", is more akin to my working class culture. I am, also, given to understand that, in this "post-modernist era" we are to tell our stories to find truth or truths in this pluralistic age. Well, this is my contribution to the truth! Amongst other perspectives I believe my story is about a struggle to make sense of God, class conflict, and difficult life events and circumstances. However, in keeping with Jesus' style, I invite you to make what you will of it. This life story is no more and no less important than other peoples' stories. But as history, for the most part, has been written by and from the viewpoint of the western middle class male, this story will be one of those that are rarely heard, because it comes out of a deeply rooted northern England working class context. Never mind the female bit!

I was born and "brought up" in a place called Ward Green, a working class council estate, situated near Barnsley. It was, and still is, a tight-knit working class community, with many people on the estate living, if not all, at lease a substantial part of their lives in Ward Green. My parents, though probably upper working class, were firmly rooted in the community, along with other relatives. It was when my friends and I, from

Diane Butler lives in the Ward Green housing estate of Barnsley. She is a Biblical Studies graduate of Sheffield University, and a member of a UTU Graduate Group.

the community, moved on to secondary school, that I realised our culture was unappreciated and often misunderstood by people outside. At secondary school I found myself in the top form while some of my friends with whom I had grown up and with whom I had a sense of oneness, were assigned to the bottom forms. They were in form 1U, which was nicknamed and known throughout the school as one useless. These friends of mine who I knew had qualities and gifts to offer were in effect written off by the education system. This was basically because their working class background had not equipped them for a middle class education.

There are many reasons why I rebelled at school, and I know that being severed from my working class friends was one of them. I didn't want to be a part of a system that could treat people like that. Fortunately, after we had been at the comprehensive school a couple of years, it went progressive. However by this time it was too late for me and I went progressively worse. For me, in this corrupt system, everyone had to fight for their rights, and justice began in the classroom or out of it. Truanting, creating havoc, and fooling around at school were the order of the day. Opting out of education allowed me to be a member of the teenage gang sub-culture of my village. I might add, this was the complete opposite to my brother who conformed and succeeded in the exam system, gaining a degree at university.

After leaving school I began work in a local light engineering factory as a quality controller. While the work was mundane, I was at home with the working class culture of the factory floor. It was very much an "us" (the factory floor workers) and a "them" (the management) atmosphere. I worked in this factory for three years and was made redundant a few months before my twenty-first birthday. I think that while factory economics played a major part in my redundancy, being asked to be shop steward only three weeks before may have contributed.

A month or so after becoming unemployed, fate struck a cruel blow. Within the space of six months my mother who had battled against cancer for five years, my father who himself had had the same fight for two years, and my only grand-parent, my grandmother, all died. As my brother, who was by now married and living down south, and the extended family became fragmented in coping with the bereavement, I was left to "pick up the pieces" of my life. I will always be indebted to my neighbours who were there for me in so many ways.

Three years after these traumatic events, at the age of twenty four, while on a one-off visit to a "full gospel" church I was "born again" in a dramatic way. God and I had been secretly communicating and trying to work things out from my teenage years. But when my parents had died I had God to "balls", and that I never wanted to speak to him again. However, in the three years of solitude that had followed bereavement, he'd had been breaking down the barriers. He, now, had swept me off my feet and bridged the great chasm between us, What was meaningful then was that I experienced God's love and the fact that he had triumphed over death. We had lost our battle against death, but this man who was God had won.

In the years following my conversion experience I was in various ways suppressed, and struggled with many tensions. My peer friends who had supported me through difficult times were unable to cope with my new found religion and disappeared from the scene. Church alienated me from my community and could not replace what I had lost. I was never really accepted or valued at church nor did I have the freedom to be myself. They were unwilling to explore my sense of calling and charismatic experiences which seemed to be confirming that calling. I think that, because I asked awkward questions and came from a working class context, this evangelical charismatic church viewed me as too much of a threat to their type of existence. In addition, I suffered conflict with their style of worship and their dogmatic belief that people who were not "born again" would go to a lost eternity. If this were true then it wrote off the whole of my family, my neighbourhood and a large number of other good people.

While Jesus remained a reality and the inner journey continued, my practical circumstances never really changed. After conversion, I was unemployed for a while, eventually securing work as a postwoman only to find that when I changed jobs I was made redundant after three weeks by my new employer. More unemployment followed until I was eventually employed by "Church Action with the Unemployed", for one year, before going on to university by mature matriculation. All this meant that I was on low income and struggled financially for several years.

Attendance at Sheffield University at the age of twenty eight, to study Biblical Studies, created more conflict. I was never fully comfortable with the middle class elitism of university, and critical study of the Bible alienated me even more from the church.

So now, I was in a position where my Biblical studies put me in tension with church, involvement with the church "cut me off" from my working class community, and my working class culture seemed irreconcilable with church and university. This situation, along with repressed grief, was all too much, and at the beginning of my third year at university I became depressed. Though depression was no stranger, to have continued my studies would have led to a total breakdown. I took a year out of university and went through eight months of counselling. I returned to finish my final year when tragedy struck again. Three weeks before the exams my uncle died. Although I was ill through bereavement when I sat my exams, and indeed was absent from one paper, I did gain the degree. Justice at last had prevailed.

2. Embracing Working Class Roots

Since then, I have made important practical and theological decisions. I realised that if Jesus does anything for us he liberates us into being ourselves. I came to the conclusion that church would never allow "me to be me", so I left. Leaving church and unemployment have caused me to retreat into my working class community and roots. These are my people and they are more important to me than belonging to church. It is by embracing my working class roots that I am free to be myself. I am once again a member of the human race, rather than a member of an archaic, irrelevant, unthinking Christianity. Leaving church has proved to be a liberating and spiritually enhancing experience.

Theologically, I have moved away from seeing the gospel in terms of personal salvation in the evangelical "born again" scheme of things. This middle class, self preserving, evangelic paradigm seems to have little room for working class people. It is unjust, oppressive and elitist. When my uncle died, I had an experience of God which conveyed that God was very much in the secular. Besides, secular people are often loving and caring. They do acts which are kingdom of God acts. Also, conversations with secular friends and neighbours indicate that they search for spirituality and struggle with God to make sense of him/her.

I have concluded that the place where I can most identify with Jesus is the place where we are at if we take what he says at face value, when he feels abandoned by God on the cross (Mk 15.34, Matt 27:46). By this I am not inferring I am forsaken by God in a "dark night of the soul" mystical or other worldly sense. I feel abandoned by God in the concrete practical realities of life. Since leaving university, I have been unemployed and live on a financial precipice. It is all about day to day survival and waiting for the next giro. I have no washing machine or television and life is bleak, with an unpromising future. The God I encounter is certainly not the God of

33

middle class Christianity. My God does not bring me worldly success, power or status nor does he liberate me from unemployment and sustained poverty. There are no rescue acts here, no deus ex machina. In this situation, in my worst moments, even a suffering God is meaningless. The middle class dominant theology of this country is found wanting in my context. I have to formulate a theology that works for me in my working class community in the 1990's. My theological agenda, then, is Who is Jesus Christ for me Today?

Living alone, unemployment is in its sixth year since leaving university. Materialistically speaking I am at the "bottom of the pile" within the community. Contact with institutionalised Christianity continues to be minimal if not bordering on the non-existent. In this situation of viewing life from the underside of history, Christ appears to have little to say in terms of the traditional radical call of the Gospel\. After all, I can hardly give up everything and live with the poor, because I am the poor - in this country at least. Neither am I out to win converts or create a church. Firstly, nobody is interested, including myself, and secondly my energies are taken up with the struggle against personal poverty. Secular parents, others, and life taught me the importance of pursuing an inner attitude of love, truth and justice. Christ affirms this, and in places sends me on the extra mile.

Discipleship, for me, can mean no other than remaining in my present context. Obviously, I need an improvement in finances, but staying in my council house isn't an act of self-denial. This is my home and I love sharing in the life of the community. All my life various aspects of society have encouraged me to move out of my context to improve my standing in the world. Christianity itself often promotes "a better life" in terms of worldly success. I never knew there was any stigma attached to living in a council house until I encountered Christianity at the age of twenty four. Middle class culture is very much a part of me now, this I wouldn't deny, and I am pleased to have had the opportunity to embrace middle class and working class cultures. Hopefully, I gain the best from both worlds. But my roots are in Ward Green, and I'm intrinsically tied to this place and its people.

It is possible to present the area as a place of despair. In the last ten years or so there has been an increase in the number of people out of work, an armed siege, a fatal stabbing, suicides, and the onset of drug pushing. However, I am aware that this gives a distorted picture, and that most of the time the majority of people enjoy what is "ordinarily" a "run of the mill" existence. Good news stories, which usually go unreported, are present in our daily life on the estate. A story, for example, of a "homeless stranger" who was "picked up" off the streets and stayed twenty-odd years in the house of a man who was bringing up two sons single-handed, only leaving when he needed professional care of the type that could only be provided by a nursing home. I think the appropriate Bible verse here is "I was a stranger and you welcomed me", Mt. 25.35. Ironically the man, a "rough diamond", who gave the stranger a home had difficulty understanding how he himself could ever be acceptable to God and church, when he smoked seventy fags a day and cursed.

Recently a group of secular blokes got together to form a football team to play a prison team down south where their friend, who many believe to be innocent, is an inmate for a date rape. The visit was so successful the authorities invited them back to a re-match. Again Mt 26.36 "I was in prison and you came to see me". This was another righteous act worthy of eternal life according to Jesus. Incidentally, when my fourteen year old dog died, some of the most consoling words came from this friend in prison. The reason I have survived poverty is largely due to the generous help of a small group of close individual Christian friends. They have eased economic burdens, welcomed me into their homes, and allowed me to participate in family life. Support is offered in many and various ways. A washing machine is their latest gift. These friends, most of whom belong to the church from which I resigned, have stuck by me when, like me, my plight has been hard to understand. The most precious gift is the friendship itself.

In the absence of wealth, profession, and status all that I can do is to learn to "be". The ordinary and mundane is special, and is where the presence of the "beyond" can be met. I want to celebrate life and our humanity. Belonging to my working class community gives identity, though ultimately God alone justifies my existence and worth. I have no idea if there is any significance or purpose to my life, it doesn't really matter and it isn't for me to know. Basically, I just want to live life immersed in the whole of life. Losing the Christian badge of identity, gained from membership of organised Christianity, has allowed this to happen.

3. What is Christianity?

This stance in life gives me the position of an insider looking out rather than, what most Christians experience, an outsider looking in on the estate. It allows me to stand with the people as one of the people. There is no difference between those living around me and myself. Perhaps it may be the case that I am more conscious of the Gospel, but this certainly doesn't make me more adept at serving the Kingdom of God. Numerous incarnational acts occur as "part and parcel" of everyday secular life. Christ resides in the secular and is represented, probably unknowingly, in the daily lives of ordinary people, as the stories I have told testify. What is more, he wasn't brought by middle class Christians trying to infiltrate the community to bring Christianity and their supposedly "better way of life" to the natives! He has always been present.

Christianity by its very nature sits over and above the secular. To become involved with institutionalised Christianity would be to rob me of my essential secularity and create a barrier with the life I seek to live in my context. Somehow religion compartmentalizes life and makes it artificial. I cannot be bothered any more to join Christian discussion groups of the type in which we go on introverted trips in the name of the gospel. I have more pressing concerns like where is the money coming from to pay the next bill or to buy food two days before the giro is due to arrive. The gospel arena, for me, is secular life and I have to get on with mine.

In my circumstances I have been fortunate that help has arisen out of friendship rather than power and dominance. As a poor person, to be seen as someone who is to be served or worked alongside is to remove further dignity, while the server gains identity and role. By having secular and Christian friends and being put in a situation where I am dependent on people, and had to learn to receive, I know how much we all need each other. Life shouts at me that liberation will never be tied up with becoming affluent. It is about recognising our interdependence rather than our independence, struggling to work out our humanity in mutuality, and having a sense of belonging. This is "what it is to be human". And I want to stake my life on these things not because Jesus tells me, though it may be the case they turn out to be what he taught and was about. It is more that I found and owned them for myself through my life experience. It is for me the right way to be in the world.

The type of discipleship that has evolved in my context, often without choice, is one in which I let go of Christian status and try to live as humanly as possible, abandoned to life, with no fixed agenda, "nurturing the moment" in Christ. I think what I am trying to describe is something similar to Bonhoeffer's ,"religionless Christianity", a kind of "naturally occurring" monasticism, spending most of my time alone, away from organised Christianity, an eremitic life in an urban setting. I would never have chosen poverty, unemployment and bereavement - they are too painful - but in them I have become aware of what is intrinsic to my humanity. I remain in my context without worldly success. The education is the exception, though it is a minor miracle in itself. I have discovered beautiful friendships, gracious practical support, and have come to appreciate the gift of life and the presence of God in the secular. Losing life I found life.

I didn't choose my context - I would never have willingly done so. Unemployment, bereavement and poverty are too painful for that. My personal theology has arisen out of my naturally occurring situation in life. What I discovered here, you might say, almost by accident, turns out to be what Jesus was teaching about. Aren't I lucky! However, I own for myself my way of life not because I learned it from Jesus or his teachings - it emerged in my own experience. I found it for myself by contemplating and reflecting about what was going off in my life. This is precisely how Jesus found it - in the 30 years of his life - out of this unrecognised life in the everyday ordinary existence of Nazereth. So it seems I have found in my context what Jesus learned in his, and later taught about. The pearl of great price, he that loses life will find it, the last shall become first, the beatitudes, the servant shall be as Lord, seem to me to say that humanity is inter-dependant and that self-abandonment is the Kingdom of God.

Jesus' findings in this context affirm what I find, and affirm my way of 'being'. He reminds me of the life I want to lead, he becomes my model, and calls me to it in the midst of the pressures of society. Being geared up for education, success, wealth, etc., is in conflict with my lifestyle. It is not what I can get out of Jesus but what He calls me to do or act. CONFLICT or Challenge is necessary to gain an improvement in living standards. If I get into a position, where I do this (get a salaried profession perhaps) the question is, can I still simply 'be' in life or will I become encumbered by possessions and live for their accumulation? Maybe I have to experience having money to deal with - then I may be able to say to Paul "I have learned, in whatever state I am, to be content." "I have learned the secret of facing plenty and hunger, abundance and want!"

Writing this paper creates conflict in me. Perhaps it defeats my way of following Christ in the world - ie getting lost in the secular and being unknown to Christianity. The problem is that theology (and what I live by) is immensely important to me, and the hardest thing in my context was having to struggle to work out my own theology, because of the dearth of theology in this country. Perhaps in telling my story, it may encourage others to find a creative, living, on-going theology for their contexts. Theology meant life or death in my context. It is what others and myself live by.

Jan Royan

NICARAGUA TO THE INNER CITY

1. From Lake District to Nicaragua

If you asked someone for directions from the Lake District to Sheffield, few people would suggest going via Nicaragua in Central America! Nevertheless, that was the rather unusual route I took in order to move from a country cottage outside Ambleside to an area of poverty the in inner city of Sheffield.

I went to Nicaragua for six weeks at the end of 1989 and the beginning of 1990 on a coffee picking brigade organised by the Nicaragua Solidarity Campaign. The Sandinista government had been in power since July 1979 struggling to exist under a Western trade embargo and a US backed campaign by the contra guerillas. Later, the February elections in 1990 were to bring down this government and the UNO party was elected which had the backing of the United States.

Looking back, even the form my visit took seems little short of miraculous because I had originally applied to go on a three week Peace Tour. It had not occurred to me that coffee picking brigades would be interested in a 46 year old woman until I read in my local paper (not renowned for its left-wing views!) of a 50 year old woman from the Lake District returning to Nicaragua to live having previously been there on a brigade. I had felt for some time that the Peace Tour was not really what I wanted - three weeks seemed too short a time to get a "feel" for the country; I did not like the idea of staying in hotels when I knew the majority of the country's people were

---

Jan Royan came to Sheffield in 1990. After the year on the Flower Estate, she moved to the St Catherine's RC Presbytery in Pitsmoor. She is a UTU Core Staff member and lecturer.

among the poorest in Latin America; and I could not see, in their programme, much time in which to meet and talk to the ordinary people, the campesinos. When I was accepted for a brigade, I felt far more certain that this was what I really wanted to do. I spent the remaining time trying to learn Spanish and reading up on Central America and a little about liberation theology.

My reasons for wanting to visit Nicaragua were largely to do with where I lived. I spent 16 years of my life in the Lake District; it was extremely beautiful and I was privileged to have lived there. But I think it was precisely because it was so beautiful, wealthy, middle-class, white and elderly that I felt driven to spend some time working and living alongside people in a part of the world where peace, wealth and privilege were almost unknown. So I went to Nicaragua, to a land of total contrast to where I lived. For there, the most immediate things that struck me were that everyone seemed young and everyone seemed poor but full of joy and hope.

Two events happened whilst I was there which have had profound significance for me, which had repercussions for my return and which still affect who I am and what I am doing.

Nicaragua

The bulk of the Coffee Brigade's time was spent on a small coffee co-operative in the north of Nicaragua, accessible only by pick-up truck along a steep and rocky path. The place was indescribably beautiful - lush, surrounded by volcanic mountains, with lots of streams. It reminded me very much of the Lake District, until I saw butterflies, bright blue and the size of my hand, or heard the whooping cries of the brightly coloured weaver birds, or the growling of the oxen and the sound of the conches which the Nicaraguans used to alert everyone that we were being moved to a different part of the coffee plantation. Although it was beautiful, it was heart-achingly poor. No sanitation, all the water was foul (we had to iodinise every drop we used), kids with swollen bellies - a sure sign of malnutrition - and very little to eat. Rice, beans, tortillas and sweet black coffee three times a day, and not much of that. Most of the Brigade were ill for part of the time there and one of our Brigade could not take the food, the rats, mice, maggots and fleas and had to leave. We started work at 6am and worked through until 3.30pm with a short break for lunch. The coffee picking itself was not too arduous but you require stamina to work such long hours. At 3.30 the ox-cart would come and we would lug our sacks of picked coffee

39

beans down the steep slopes so that they could be weighed at the medida at the end of each day.

Our Brigade of 16 stayed in the schoolhouse, the largest building on the co-op. The school was closed for the whole of the coffee harvest, so that even the young boys of eight upwards could help pick, for coffee was the life-blood of that community. At the end of the first week, I was invited by Teresa to go and live in her house for the rest of my time there. She and five other members of her family lived in a house the size of an average English living room, with a dirt floor. They managed to squeeze me in by putting up a home-made, rickety camp bed every night and I slept with mice skittering around the bag of maize at my head, and a broody hen and her chicks at my feet and got bitten to death by fleas. Every drop of water had to be carried up from the stream, about half a mile away and up the side of a mountain, and to go to the loo you squatted down in the field next door. But I loved it and I was incredibly happy with them all.

Despite my limited Spanish, Teresa and I spent hours talking to each other, with the aid of a dictionary, a Spanish New Testament (she was a devout Catholic) and lots of laughter and sometimes tears. One of the things I did when I went out to Nicaragua was to take with me photographs of my family and my life in the Lake District. With only limited Spanish, it is surprising how much contact you can make using photographs. One of the photos I had taken with me was of the stone-built cottage I used to live in in the Lake District. It was not my cottage, it went with the job I did, and it was small by Lake District standards, but to the Nicaraguans at La Pita it was a palace. So, frequently in the evenings at Teresa's house, she would ask to see the photos and the one she gazed at most often was the one of the cottage. How many people lived in it? Just me! How many rooms did it have? What was in each of the rooms? What did I do in each room? And then she looked at the tumbled down shed next to the house. Now this shed was in such a state of disrepair and was so damp that I only kept wood for the fire in it. But the first time Teresa saw the photograph she said to me, looking at the shed, "And who lives in that house?" And I was so ashamed of all the wealth, the choice, the sheer unimaginable amount of space and luxury allotted just to me that I wanted to rush immediately back to the Lake District and go and live in that shed.

We spent Christmas and New Year on the co-op and it was the best Christmas of my life - totally simple with a mass celebrated by a visiting Mexican Jesuit priest on Christmas Eve and the luxury of meat. They killed two of the co-op pigs and used everything except for the bristles.

It was hard leaving Teresa and all the children on the co-op, but from there we went to Matagalpa, the nearest large town, to a series of political/social meetings we had requested. Somehow an additional meeting was slipped in that we had not asked for, a meeting with the Mothers of Heroes and Martyrs of the Revolution.

So our Brigade, together with a Canadian one, got herded together into a small room in stifling heat, expecting to be given another rousing speech by some Sandinista bigwigs. (We had had quite a lot of them by this time and were getting a bit fed up with them.) But this was different. It was a short talk given by some women who had all lost sons, fathers, husbands and brothers - some of them every male member of their family - either during the Revolution in 1979 or in the contra war that followed it.

These women had been displaced because their homes had been destroyed by the contra and they had all come to a barrio on the edge of Matagalpa where they had to learn to survive in a manless environment (and Nicaragua has no Welfare State). So they formed themselves into a community, growing vegetables co-operatively, and mending, washing and selling clothes donated by a Swedish organisation. They met to read a passage from the Bible and to reflect on it in the light of their own lives and suffering. They were all Catholics except Paulina, a tiny 55 year old woman, who sat next to me. At one point she piped up that she was "evangelica" - a Protestant - but she joined in with the Bible study and believed that Jesus was with them in their struggle.

Then one of the women read a poem she had written and another sang a song commemorating the deaths of their sons and at this point Paulina started to cry. She had lost two sons and her husband in the Revolution. I was sitting on the floor nearest to her and although she was sobbing bitterly nobody else seem to take any notice. I am ashamed to say at this point I hesitated, but thank God, not for long and I just put out my hand and held hers. And it was like an electric current between us. She grasped my left hand tightly and eventually stopped crying.

At the end we were all invited to visit the barrio where these women lived and Paulina grabbed my arm and clung on to me and talked all the way up the steep track. At one point, I told her that I, too, was "evangelica" and had many Catholic friends. So she had to stop and kiss me for that and when we got to the barrio I was treated like a queen and invited into all her friends' house where often the one and only stool was dusted for me to sit on.

They had nothing to offer me to eat or drink but water (and never drink untreated Matagalpa water came into my mind) as I sipped my third plastic cup of it, but their delight in my visit was totally overwhelming. It was completely over the top, out of all proportion and unexpected. At the end I knew that this was why I was in Nicaragua - to feel with the women part of the pain and joy of their struggle in the ongoing Revolution. Seven years later it is still vividly etched in my heart and mind.

2. From Nicaragua to the Flower Estate

A week later I flew back to Heathrow and returned to the Lake District. But that brief visit to Nicaragua, although it physically ended in January 1990, continued to resonate in my life. And like yeast working away in bread or wine, it affected me and caused me to question and to make changes in my life.

Do you remember Teresa's question "And who lives in that house?" meaning the rickety shed? I came back to the Lake District with that question reverberating in my mind. And I looked out of my bedroom window across a field to a huge white mansion with at least eight bedrooms which was lived in by a Dutch heart specialist and his wife for no more than six weeks of the year. And I thought about my near neighbour who owned a house in Lancashire and a nearby barn converted into a holiday home, and a very recently acquired small cottage near to it - bought because he did not know what sort of person might otherwise buy it. And I thought of Teresa. And I looked at my 16 years of living in the Lake District, and the cottage I lived in, a mansion by Nicaraguan standards, and asked why?

It was not that the owner of the big white mansion or my near neighbour there were evil people, but that the structures in which they lived (and I believe in which they were trapped), the structures in which I and we all live allows some people to have three houses and some people in the world only a shack, or none. Even in this country. And it is hard and painful and difficult to allow these questions to surface and to let the answers become the reality out of which we are forced to act.

In the end, I knew that to be true to God, to myself, to Teresa and Paulina, and to the many other Teresas and Paulinas of this world, I could no longer with a clear conscience continue living in my secure, beautiful, white, wealthy, middle-class part of the world. That somehow, however irrational and ill-thought out, it was right for me to come and live in an inner city, and so I came to Sheffield.

The Flower Estate

I came with two friends from the Lake District to live in the Wincobank Chapel House, on the Flower Estate, an area of poverty in north-east Sheffield. Most of the people living in the mainly council housing around us were marginalised - poor, unemployed and many of them were single parents, often victims of abuse and violence. From the start, the three of us said that we wanted to live in an open house, so that the kids from the surrounding estate (and some of the parents) were free to come and go for most of the day and the evening. We played games with them, baked bread and cakes (I still make Hector cake, named after one of the kids on the estate), played the piano and just talked with them. They thought we were totally weird because we ate strange food (vegetarian) around a table, we bought most of our clothes from charity shops or jumble sales, we did not possess a video, microwave or even a colour TV, we went to church and were not "spooked" by the Victorian Undenominational Chapel next door, and we even went into it on our own at night. But mainly we were weird or different because we talked to them and listened to them and did not shout at them all the time. We treated them with respect.

After a while they stopped treating us as aliens from outer space and we settled into a routine with them. But retrospectively, I realise that my attitude towards the people on the estate was what I would term colonialist. I had come to give them something, to help them. Iit was a small and unexpected experience that showed me what liberation they could offer to me.

The gift I particularly value was given to me by a 12 year old girl, whom I shall call Jenny. The couple with whom I shared the house had gone away for the weekend. One dark, wet, cold November night I came home from work to find Jenny wet and shivering on the doorstep (she was inadequately dressed as were most of the children on the estate). She greeted me with the news that my friends' cat had been killed by two dogs who had cornered her, partly at the instigation of their owners, and torn her throat. She said she would show me where the cat was and we found her, stiff and cold and very dead, lying in the darkest part of the land surrounding the house. I said I would have to bury her and Jenny said she would help.

Armed with pick and shovel and getting wetter and colder by the minute, we attacked the rockhard clay with our implements and managed eventually to dig a shallow hole. I fetched a towel and plastic bag and we put Topsy into it and buried her. By this time, I was crying. Topsy had been part of my life, too, in the Lake District and I could imagine how the family would feel when they returned home and heard how she had died. Jenny put her arms around me and said "Don't cry, Jan. Topsy's happy now". Then to prevent dogs from digging up Topsy's body, we lugged heavy stones to lay over the grave.

When I thought we had got enough, I turned to Jenny and said, "That'll do. Let's go in and get warm and have a cup of tea." It was Jenny who said, very hesitantly, "Shouldn't we say a prayer for Topsy, Jan?". And that made me cry again at the thought of this girl, who had rarely set foot in church, who had been taken into care, known what it was like to bear the brunt of violence done to herself, her sisters and her mother, teaching me about the love of God for all creation.

And the next day, it was Jenny, her sister and two of their friends, who helped me to clear up all the broken glass and the mess left in the chapel next door after it had been broken into yet again.

In Nicaragua, our Brigade had several opportunities to meet and talk to teachers, doctors and health workers, as well as visiting hospitals, a prison, the Human Rights organisation plus a full political programme run for visiting brigadistas. We were encouraged to talk to anyone and everyone and, as well as meeting many FSLN (Sandinista) supporters, we also encountered people who supported one of the opposition parties.

I stayed on the Flower Estate in Sheffield for nearly a year and during my time there I got to know one of the local GPs quite well and he willingly gave up time to talk to me about health problems associated with an area of poverty. I also spent several months acting as a volunteer teacher for half a day each week at the local primary school and thus had many opportunities of observing the level of education of Flower Estate children.

As a result of these two experiences, I decided to look at both societies in parallel and to try and draw some conclusions about differences and similarities in Nicaraguan and Flower Estate society.

3. Nicaragua and the Flower Estate

Parallels between The Flower Estate, Sheffield
and La Pita Co-operative, Nicaragua

Flower Estate | La Pita

Poverty

Quite marked in some houses but more based on lack of education, i.e. knowing how to manage on a low income. In some families it is evidenced by poor diet and little furniture. In others quite a high income but it is often spent before the next Giro is due.

Intense, but in the country and on the co-op everyone was poor, and having land to cultivate and harvest was wealth for many families. Poverty was more obvious in the cities where small children would be trying to sell chewing gum and cigarettes. Actually saw a shack on the outskirts of Managua made entirely of cardboard boxes. There is no Welfare State benefit.

Clothing

Children often dressed in totally inadequate and dirty clothes, even at school. Often the clothes they wear would have been quite expensive initially. Much use is made of buying clothes from catalogues. Seems to be an embargo on getting even good quality secondhand clothes. Oxfam is definately "out". Footwear is frequently grossly inappropriate for weather conditions.

Neither adults nor children had many clothes and often what they had were ragged and dirty. Young children often went bare-bottomed as nappies are expensive and in short supply. Little evidence of warm clothes to combat the sometimes chilly winds and very few people had clothing against rain. They wrapped plastic sheets around themselves. Many young children were bare-footed.

Diet

Most food is junk/fast food. Lots of chips, sweets, pop and cheap meat. Kids are incredibly fussy about what they like and don't like and seldom seem to have a proper meal. Baking seems unheard of. Most meals eaten either standing up or watching TV, except for Sunday lunch. On Sundays, most families seem to have a roast, Yorkshire pud. and veg. and there is more of an effort to eat together. Local Health Centre very keen to promote diet among mums. Chapel House was very popular among the kids for an opportunity to bake bread and cakes and to comment on the vegetarian food eaten there.

Fortunately the basic diet of the Nicaraguans in the country is healthy - rice, beans & maize tortillas eaten 3 times a day. But green veg are considered fit only for animals and most Nicas are cautious about eating anything different. Meat is a real treat - eaten only rarely. Individual families ate the occasional chicken and eggs and a very salty cheese. Sweet black coffee is the staple drink and both adults and children chew sugar cane, so their teeth aren't too good. At the co-op we ate meat communally only once, pork on Christmas Eve.

Health

Flower Estate highest prescribing area in Sheffield. Very high rate of depression and many women on high dosage of anti-depressants. General health very poor despite great efforts by local Health Centre to foster awareness. Heavy smoking, drinking, some drug taking and lack of knowledge of basic health care. Very high incidence of women abused as children and this therefore makes adult relationships difficult. High incidence of

Some evidence of real ignorance, eg with sanitation, water and health. Much evidence of malnutrition in young children. Young children still die of diarrhoea and vomiting because mothers won't follow basic oral rehydration instructions. But Health Service has only existed since 1979 and in remote areas there are insufficient health workers. Vaccination and immunisation programmes were very successful. Introduction of prescription charges life-related disease, eg. cervical cancer, heart disease, alcohol related illness.

are making poorer people unable to avail themselves of Health Service. Growing interest in herbal medicine.

Education

Lipservice is paid to the importance of it by parents, but often they actively encourage their children to "wag it off school". Significantly low numbers attended a Parents Evening at local Middle School. Reading Age of many F.E. children is extremely low and it is quite common for 10-11 year old children to be unable to read words of one syllable. Parents frequently say they would like something better for their children but fail to see the importance of their own role in promoting their children's education.

Nicaragua was awarded the UNESCO prize for improving the illiteracy level - from 50% down to 13%. At La Pita, education was rated so highly that they paid themselves for a teacher to come and live on the co-op to teach their children as their numbers were too low to warrant receiving a paid Government teacher. Very moving to be with adults who have only recently learnt to read. Because of inflation and the economic situation at end of 89/90 teachers' pay was very low and they had to receive a Government food subsidy to survive. Children attend school from 6-14.

Families

According to local GP, very high incidence of early teenage pregnancy. But having children is seen as an occupation and something that gives young women status and prestige. Most women seem genuinely fond of babies but their lack of good mothering role models and the instability of their relationships causes tensions as children grow older. Quite common for early teenage children to move out into extended family, the girls often returning home when pregnant. Not uncommon to have 4-6 children in family, often by several different fathers. Quite frequent for one child almost to live at a friend's house for days on end and only move home when there is a row and a subsequent break-up of friendship. Family loyalty is very important. Because of size of families and small houses children frequently have to share rooms and sometimes beds, making privacy difficult. Because of the size of families and the adult male partner often not being the father of all (or even any) of the children, very high incidence of child abuse.

Children grow up very young in Nica. At 12/13 you are an adult and quite often a parent. 8-10 year old boys will almost do a man's work and same age girls will have 2-3 younger children to look after. Both boys and girls accept this quite uncomplainingly. Often both parents work full-time during the coffee harvest, women getting up at 2-3am to work in the communal kitchen and not finishing till 5pm. Families can be enormous by British standards with 6-15 kids quite common although now stabilising at 9-10. Children are security for old age in a country with no State pension scheme. Also although contraception and sterilisation are freely available, orthodox Catholic teaching forbids them. Few demands for abortion in a country where children are doted on; although it is illegal, it is still easily obtainable. No fostering or adoption for orphaned kids, of which there are many, as this is automatic by the extended family. Early teenage pregnacy the norm. Still a strong macho image for young men, although the FSLN Government was trying to change that. 30,000 young men killed between 1980-89.

Religious Beliefs

I didn't meet one single family who regularly attended church and who actually lived on the Flower Estate. Because taught religion is mainly missing in both homes and schools, children have little or no concept of God or Jesus. Nevertheless, there was a great deal of spirituality around and, it seemed to me, a desire to have some kind of religious belief but not necessarily church-based. Superstition

Nicaragua is a predominantly Catholic country but the church was totally split between the right wing faction headed by the orthodox Cardinal Obando y Bravo and the left wing, liberation theology & FSLN supporters. The FSLN had 4 practising priests in its Government. There are few churches in the rural areas, but there didn't seem to be any shortage of priests. Base Christian communities played quite a large part - ghosts, hauntings, spiritualism, astrology, and a "God killed my rabbit" belief in an avenging policeman God.

exist in large towns. Very strong emphasis on religious festivals, particularly those connected with Virgin Mary and saints. Strong Protestant Moravian church on the east coast and a steadily growing Pentecostal church.

Environmental Concerns

The vandalism and litter on the estate are extreme. Dogs are normally left to roam the streets and foul the area all the time. Children systematically destroy empty houses, trees, cars, telephone boxes, although there is a code of honour about not wrecking property belonging to people they know. Although children are taught about the environment at school, it appears to have little or no impact on their lifestyle. As the children are seldom treated with respect by their parents or anyone else, it is perhaps idealistic to expect them to treat the environment with respect.

Until 1979, US logging companies systematically denuded large areas of Nicaragua, so reafforestation was a major task for the FSLN Government. The environment has gradually become an area of awareness for the Government, but much needs to be done. The Environmental Network for Nica has been set up there and abroad and funds are being sought to do many necessary projects, for example, cleaning up the vastly polluted Lake Managua. Esteli has a very large herb farm for alternative medicines and people are actively encouraged to take an interest in their immediate environment. The major problem is still lack of clean and safe water.

Violence and Drunkeness

It's very common for both men and women to get very drunk, usually in the pub. Often see really young children and even babies in pushchairs hanging around outside the pubs and clubs during the day and even late at night. Whilst I lived there, a young man was stabbed to death in the next road - a crime passionel brought on by jealousy, drugs and drink. There is a lot of violence done to women - abuse, rape, and beatings are commonplace. Every house consistently shows violent videos and all ages watch them. The kids - girls and boys - fight all the time. Some glue-sniffing, but not much evidence of hard drugs.

It is the norm on Saturdays for the men to get totally legless and just fall down in a stupor wherever they happen to be. Because of the contra threat, AKA guns are easily available and one hears many stories of people injuring themselves and others (usually accidentally) because of playing around with weapons whilst drunk. The women don't drink at all. AMNLEA (the Women's Movement) say there is violence done to women and incest is quite common. Local drink is rum, brewed on the co-op - very strong and very lethal.

Privacy

The noise levels were incredibly high but it didn't seem to disturb most people. Silence and quiet speaking are unheard of. Adults yell at the kids and the kids yell back to them and to each other. In most houses, the radio, TV and loud music were on simultaneously and it was often difficult for me to hear what people were saying. Adults and children were in and out of each other's houses all day long and few people were ever alone. The size of the families make solitude a comparative rarity and rooms were nearly always shared and by choice children often shared beds. They thought I was mad because I liked to be alone.

At La Pita the houses were minute yet they managed to squeeze me in on a home-made camp bed in a house already containing 7 people, the size of an average living room. There is no recognition of the need for privacy and because we were objects of curiosity, we were never left alone by the children. The noise on the co-op was of a different dimension from that of the city - animals and children mainly. Even so, the cockerels and dogs made sleeping at night difficult. Children often sleep 2, 3 or even 4 to a bed and in such small houses, the most intimate acts are conducted with no privacy at all.

There were not many signs of hope overtly displayed on the Flower Estate, but many signs of anger and a lot of apathy. Most parents expressed a hope that life for their children would be better then it was for them, although realistically few parents did much to give that hope much credance, i.e. through an interest in their children's education. Their solidarity was very "clan" based - you don't grass to the police; you get what you can from the "caring" professions, but ultimately it's what you can get out of society for you and yours. Nevertheless, among the women there was a very genuine support system in terms of lending and borrowing money; child-care; and listening to each other's problems. Gossip about each other was the life-blood of their conversation.

The people we met at La Pita, and elsewhere in Nicaragua tended to be supporters of the FSLN, so it was not surprising that they felt proud of the Revolution. Many women had sacrificed much for its sake, but although all of them longed for peace and an end to conscription, I did not hear one woman speak against the gains of the Revolution; mostly they had moved from landless campesinos to being people with hope. On the surface, there seemed to be a lot of support by the local people for the local FSLN party, but since Feb. 1990 this was proved not to be the case. As far as solidarity between each other on the co-op was concerned, this seemed very strong - both for the whole co-op with men and women working together to bring in the coffee harvest and between the women working together in the kitchen.

Pride

I think the families on the F.E. were utterly typical of the family quoted by Jeremy Seabrook in his book "The Race for Riches" i.e. that you demonstrated your love for your family according to what you bought them and how much it cost. To my "refined and middle-class" mind, a lot of what they bought seemed to me to be tasteless, over-priced and shoddy. But spending literally hundreds of pounds on their kids via the catalogues at Christmas time was the way the F.E. parents expressed their love. Their pride was in having everything that was the latest fashion, what the TV ads told them would give them pleasure and satisfaction.

Nicaraguans seemed to express their pride in 2 ways:
1. by commemorating those who had died either in the Revolution or in the Contra war in a variety of emotional and often ostentatious ways, and
2. by ensuring that at whatever cost their children had as good an education as they could get for them. At times of fiesta, they would dress them up in their Sunday best. The contrast between the ragged clothes of the children on the Co-op most of the time and the frilly light coloured dresses the girls wore at Christmas was really marked. And this in a country without washing machines and washing powder.

4. UTU and After

There is one further outcome from my Teresa-And who lives in that house?, holding-Paulina's-hand, Jenny's-Shouldn't we say a prayer for Topsy? and my attempt to seek parallels between La Pita and the Flower Estate. A year after I came back from Nicaragua and was living in Sheffield, I did the Diploma in Theology and Mission on the Study Year at the Urban Theology Unit in Sheffield. One of the speakers on Liberation Theology was a Catholic priest, called Gerry Burke. He had spent several years in a poor barrio in Lima and came to talk to us of his experience there. He told us that shortly after his arrival in Lima, he became ill and went to see a Peruvian doctor. This doctor told him, "Your head tells you that you have come over here to do a job. Your heart tells you that you do not love these people. If you cannot love them, go home, because you will only harm yourself and them unless you can love them". He stayed and grew to love and respect the Peruvian people deeply. What was profoundly shocking to me was that this middle-aged priest told this to us all, a group of total strangers, with tears in his eyes. He openly and visibly and without the slightest embarrassment revealed his own vulnerability to us. He then carried on to give us a brilliant and objective account of Paolo Frere's process of liberation theology. But I felt as though the earth had rocked beneath my feet.

And irrationally, responding only to some deeply felt need in myself, I wanted to tell him and the rest of the group about Paulina. So, instead of doing my carefully worked out talk on Boff's liberation theology, that is what I did. At the end of the day, John Vincent, the Director, was winding up. Suddenly, Gerry Burke said, "Just a minute, John". And he looked at me and said "Which hand did you hold Paulina's with, Jan?". "My left", I said. He walked across the room, took my left hand and said, again with tears in his eyes, "Thank you for loving her". And without knowing how or why, the circle was complete. Gerry's act of solidarity, his recognition, his validation and affirmation helped me to move on from the Flower Estate and a long phase of my life to reach out in trust to the next stage.

5. Reflection

Six years later on, I look back and wonder what the theology behind all this is. I think three points have emerged in my understanding and experience of the theology of liberation.

First, the people of our 20th century world are no quicker to understand than the disciples of Jesus were, so the process of liberation and the theology that develops from it is always a learning process, ongoing and open to change. Nobody ever reaches a state of total liberation (well, not in this life) and because the theology of liberation must come from reflection on experience, then we feel first and understand later. Like the disciples on the road to Emmaus, our hearts burn within us (we feel and experience) but we do not recognise (reflect and understand) until after the event. So, liberation theology is vitally concerned with "doing" and "experiencing" theology rather than it being an academic or spiritual study primarily, even if the "doing" only involves an act of consciously placing oneself in a different place, of "being" there. Unlike a theoretic, scientific approach to life, liberation theology develops its belief systems on concrete experience and feelings.

Second, there is a saying attributed to the aborigines:

"If you have come to help me, you are wasting your time. But if you have come because your liberation is bound up with mine, then come, let us walk together."

Liberation theology is not colonialist or involved in imposing structures, aid or development on a group or class of people. Its origin must come from the authentic felt experience of people in a specific context. Their liberation from the yoke of oppression may help to liberate those who have seen that their own liberation is bound up with others. It can be a process of continuous conversion where mutual empowering and evangelisation can take place.

All societies have some forms of underclass and "top dog" class and recognising that being marginalised, voiceless and powerless to change and to choose is not what the Kingdom of God is about is the first important step in recognising and then fighting to lift oppressive structures.

Liberation theology is about empowering people to shake off the yoke of oppression because God does not desire any one of his people to live lives of sub-human indignity. It is liberation to the poor because it reveals to them that grinding, abject poverty is as abhorrent to God as it is degrading to them. Equally important, though, is the acceptance that every human being in any society has the power to oppress and is also a victim of oppression.

Finally, the theology of liberation is both individual and community based. Luke 4 has Jesus proclaiming good news to the poor. But Jesus goes on to say that he brings freedom to prisoners and sight to the blind, as well as removing the yoke of oppression. We are all of us blind, dumb and captive to our compulsions, unable to recognise, let alone escape from, our slavery to obsessive behaviour and the structures of sin which bind us to evil ways of living. In John 10.10, Jesus tells us that he has come in order to give us life, "life in all its fullness". Most of our lives we are oppressed and we oppress others by not acting out of our authentic selves, the self that is made in the image and likeness of God and which is all humankind's common inheritance.

So, liberation theology needs to be as much for the rich as it is for the poor, perhaps more so because the rich have far more they need to be liberated from. What oppresses people who are wealthy is their status, their desire to protect and defend their material gains and their independent and selfish ways of living. It is metanoia, conversion, freedom, to recognise that those things we have clung to to save us from death are in fact the weapons of death, of slavery. It is only when we are faced with a sense of the intolerable in our lives, die some kind of death to the selfishness of our ego, that we can rise to the power of becoming our true selves, the authentic liberated person God calls us to be.

Margaret Hebblethwaite, writing recently about base ecclesial communities (BECs) in Australia says:

"So once again the phenomenon can be observed that has been commented on so often in the Third World: BECs are formed most easily among the poorer sections of society. Ruth's (Ruth Egar, a Mercy Sister) explanation is that "there is an energy and a great generosity among those who have less to lose. As we get more into the middle class, as materialism grabs us more, we become less able and less willing to want to belong. And belonging to community is what it is all about." (The Tablet, May 1996)

The poor of this world can help us on this road to liberation by revealing how we oppress them, calling on us to join with them in a mutual search for the bond that unites us all in our common humanity. Through the theology of liberation, Jesus Christ reveals to us the face of God calling us to work together for his kingdom of justice, peace and love.

Linda Granville

I AM A SINGLE PARENT

1. Take a Good Look at Me

Well, here I am.   Take a good look. I am the cause of this country's economic decline. I am a single parent.

I'm not in the category of the widowed. I'm not in the category of the divorced. I belong to that grey area that has two children each with different fathers and I've never been married. And those fathers, through their own choice, have never had any contact whatsoever, virtually from the day I told them I was pregnant. I have two beautiful girls aged 16 and 12 and we love each other dearly.

I suppose there are some people in this room who might judge me at different degrees. And I have been judged - from areas that even I didn't realise. But you couldn't have judged me more than I judged myself at the time. My main concern was God couldn't possibly love me now. He could forgive me once, but not quite as much the second time. But then I read a passage from the Bible, Romans 8, verse 30:

> It began: "If God is for us, who can be against us" and it finished: "Nothing in all creation can separate me from the love of God in Christ Jesus".

From that moment I knew that whatever condition I was in. God stood beside me, loved me, accepted me. I could hold up my head with anybody. And I'm convinced that the same goes for any marginalised person   in   this

Linda Granville has worked for several years with Respond in Middlesborough and has more recently been active in Church Action on Poverty Hearings, at one of which the talk here was first given.

society. My task was to convince some members of the church, some members of my family, some members of society of that, and ten years on, I find I still have to convince the government. The line in the St Francis prayer "Seek ye not to be loved, but to love", was my way forward.

"Single parents only get pregnant to get a roof over their heads," I was told. Fourteen years of really hard work flashed before my eyes. The sad part was that it had trickled down from government to some close friends too. It has made me acutely sad, but angry. Why should I start proving myself to society, yet again, after years of coming through emotional trauma, of isolation, of learning to value myself?

I have to say that I do appreciate my council house. I got it after living with my mother for two years after my first child was born. I was lucky that then I got a grant for basic necessities such as a cooker etc. I'll never forget a mother of a single parent sobbing her eyes out over the phone to me asking where she could find second hand furniture quickly because she hadn't the room to take in her daughter to live with her and the daughter was due out of hospital with a new baby but had nothing in her council flat but bare boards. She had no bed, no cot, no chair to sit on, no cooker, nothing even to heat the new baby's food.

I felt deeply sad for the new single parents who would have to take all this prejudiced rubbish on board, knowing they had enough to contend with, with a lifetime's commitment of selfless struggle. And if that's the price to pay for a roof over your head then society has a lot to answer for. And I'd put it to you that especially in this climate of three generations unemployed in some areas, and all the relationship problems that that entails, it's not so much a roof, but it's non-judgmental love that all of us are looking for, and single parents are no different from anybody else.

One of the most important jobs in our society is to bring up a child and it is the most underestimated. I had my children late in life. I had years of coping on my own twenty four hours a day with screaming babies with only my wonderful seventy-year old mum to help. For years I had only four or five hours sleep a day. Since my children started school and had to pay bus fares, I have only ever once, in all those years, taken the three of us down town together on the bus.

Although I've always been honest and upfront, I have in the past been summoned to the DSS office and seriously threatened with prison because I was living on my family allowance for two weeks, saving my income support for the winter bills. They thought I had a paid job on the side, "How could anybody live on such a low income?", they said. I later received a full apology.

It was important to keep a safe family environment for my children, so I took a part-time job to top up my income support. I was greatly exploited as a part-time cleaner, taking home £2.50 per hour - less than the basic hourly rate because I could not earn more than £15 per week. Two people were sacked and I and a few others were left to cover their work - cleaning urine and vomit in men's toilets - with no extra pay. I had to leave my children with my mother on a Christmas night so I could get to work the next morning. When I finally reached work, not one of the staff had turned up. They all had hangovers from the staff party the night before. I wasn't even asked to attend the party.

According to the 1991 census, there are 50,400 women part-time workers in Cleveland.

At the same time, I was voluntarily running a teenage drop-in centre, helping the handicapped, teaching English to Asian women, interviewing and writing about grass roots community groups around Cleveland. I represented the unemployed at the European Parliament in Strasbourg - yet I allowed myself to be exploited for the sake of £15.

I've spoken about this in the past, but the struggle continues. Recently I became really acutely miserable when years of living with this constant heavy drone of worrying where the next penny was coming from caught up with me. I know I work very hard in the voluntary work I do. Where is the balance in all of this? A friend innocently and predictably asked, "Why don't you get a full-time paid job?" I went to bed and sobbed my heart out.

I tried to analyse why I was crying. Why do people put so much store in gaining money as a measure of our value in society? Why do we continue to bang our heads against a brick wall and look for a money solution when evidence shows that money is not reaching the poor in this trickle down economic system? The only thing that does trickle down is fear, and it goes from top to bottom - fear of losing government positions, fear of losing a business, fear of losing jobs, fear of losing what little money we have, fear of losing dole.

Fear is poverty.

2. Take a Deeper Look at Me

I know that I have values gained through 16 years of being a single parent. Being in a poverty trap has enabled me to throw away the thought of ever having money and this has been the key to my growth as a person. Money has not been the driving force in the things that I do. This has opened up new values in me, namely that my value is not in what I take from this planet, but in the things that I give. I have a sense of freedom to be who I am. I have a choice in the voluntary work that I do to reach my full potential as a human being. I am rich indeed. And although it is a very heavy price to pay, all the money in the world can't buy that. In any case, even if I did get a full-time paid job, who would look after my children?

It still leaves millions of unemployed people out in the cold. I would like to think that the work that I do values those people and promotes their values. Part of that work is to be part of the core group that helped arrange this conference and I think that's a worthwhile thing to do - more so than being exploited as a part-time worker cleaning up vomit in the men's toilets.

I want to say thank you to all the very special people who have, over the years, given me practically every stick of furniture in my house. I want to say thanks to all those charity-shop workers who give their time freely for nothing so I can dress decently and not be in danger of losing benefit for going to a job interview scruffily dressed. At this point I have to give special thanks to my 80-year old mam for her sense of love and laughter which has seen me through many a traumatic period, and, along with my friends at Respond, from the early years has stood beside me, accepted me as I am, listened, supported, trusted and loved me. I've been blessed. But what about those with no support whatsoever?

Whole communities are floundering under the constant heavy drip of the trickle down money economy. It doesn't have to be like this. The true wealth of any community lies in the talents and resources of its people, so when I first heard of Local Exchange and Trading Systems (Lets), it was like an answer to prayer. People put their goods or God-given talents into a central pool and take from the pool goods they need or expertise to get jobs done that normally they probably could not afford. It all works without the use of money.

It started about 12 years ago in Canada and there are about 200 systems currently all over Britain. Instead of money, Cleveland Lets uses the "doofer". A doofer has no physical existence. It is simply a way of keeping track of what we give and what we receive. Basic to Cleveland Lets is the revaluing of people - the revaluing of women's work, of children, of the elderly, of the carers, of the unemployed. Instead of one doofer equalling a pound, five doofers equals one hour of anybody's work. Hence Cleveland Lets Motto is "Lets doofer each other".

We can tap into such things as trips to the Lake District - and for a single parent, to have a trip out once in a blue moon with your children is a virtual God-send. All kinds of things can be pooled - walking the dog, tuition in almost anything, aromatherapy massage, going messages for a neighbour, a bed for the night ... your imagination is the limit. A whole wealth of people-resource is being revealed and people are finally valuing themselves in the ordinary things they do every day.

However, I am exasperated and exhausted because according to a government ruling, people on benefits on a Lets system could be penalised. An immense mountain of untapped people-talent is wasted. This is poverty. In Australia the government encourages Lets and promotes it as "people looking for employment".

What channel have I got now to promote my values to my children? Can you imagine how schizophrenic I feel when I go round the community promoting something that I whole heartedly believe in, about which the unemployed shout "Great", about which the disabled shout "Great", and then I have to say "But hang on, it's for everybody else, but not for you". We must get it into our brains that the world economy has a wider aspect than only money.

To conclude. Every single one of us has a small part to play. As a parent, for the sake of all our children, I would like to ask each and every one of you to look within yourself and, if you must insist on sticking to the trickle down economy, let generosity trickle down instead of greed, let truth trickle down instead of closing your eyes to reality. Let standing beside your fellow man or woman in whatever condition he or she is trickle down instead of bigotry. Let hope trickle down instead of suicidal hopelessness. Let love trickle down and let the fear of poverty disappear for ever.

Moby Farrands

GOSPEL STORIES IN RADFORD

1. Eschatology and Uncleanness

Inner City - and End Times

The issues in inner city Radford, in Nottingham, where I work, tend to carry a depressingly repetitive negative message. There is much of the usual inner city mix - poverty, unemployment, broken and single families, poor housing, homelessness, powerlessness and injustice. There is more about wilderness and crucifixion here than signs of resurrection. To look for signs of hope I have to look at individuals swimming against an unstoppable tide.

The information that the redistribution of wealth is now going into reverse is no surprise in Radford, where the gap between the lifestyle of the affluent people we see working in the city centre and the lifestyles of most Radford people become more and more starkly distinct. Every new Government decision seems to work against Radford people, whether it is the new written tests for seven year-olds which will label our children as failures, or the wretched City Challenge initiatives which mean that impoverished city areas are set in competition against each other. The preparation of bids takes money, skill and energy that could have been used for our communities.

Areas where brave struggles were going on seem to be crushed by circumstances or Government legislation. Individuals who have fought against the tide seem to be broken by being discredited, or succumbing to

---

Moby Farrands is a Community Worker based at the Radford Community House, and works in the inner city area of Nottingham. She is a tutor with the Diploma in Community Ministry course at UTU.

petty corruption, or exhausted by the struggle to fight for other people and not for themselves, even though they are also in need.

I have a lot of sympathy with my black Pentecostal friends who look to the end times described by Jesus in Matthew 24 or by St John in Revelations. The end of the world has come in the inner city!

Momtaz - and the Unclean Woman

When I first met Momtaz she was permitted to see me by her Bangladeshi husband only because I was English and middle class, not like the local Pakistani, Bengali or Indian families whom he considered peasants. He had broken off all contact with Islam, very rare behaviour in our neighbourhood, and had insulted all of his Asian neighbours. She was pregnant, unhappy and scared because she knew her husband was dying. She had four young sons. I convinced her husband that Momtaz needed English lessons, and there at last she made a few Asian friends.

When he died, I listened to her grief, found help for her and her children from church volunteers while she had her baby and helped her to sort out her financial affairs. All these things, like physical healing, helped, but she still felt alone, despite my friendship.

Shameem, a Pakistani friend, suggested that I take her along to her Muslim women's prayer group two roads away. Although none were from Bangladesh, they made us very welcome in their family atmosphere. A mum from the group then visited her every week, attempting to communicate through a similar language barrier to mine.

I found out about a children's weekly Bengali language and Koran reading class linked to a Bengali women's group. Shameem got her husband to take Momtaz and her five children to the group. After a few weeks, a Bangladeshi dad volunteered to fetch her. At last Momtaz knew she had new women to be her sisters, to share her worries and joys. She had a new extended family. She had achieved what we had wished for her - "Shalom", peace and wholeness within her own community.

Momtaz's return to completeness makes a link for me with the sick woman in Mark 12. 25-34, who had bled for twelve years, making her unclean within traditional Jewish culture, but whom Jesus restored to communal acceptability. Or the lepers throughout the Gospels whom Jesus returned to their community through healing.

2. Strange Allies

Alan - The One not against us

The " 4B's" Tenants Association has represented many parables and Gospel images to me in its eventful history. In the beginning I saw the parable of the sower and the seed in Matthew 13. 3-8 as relevant. When my United Reformed Church colleagues and I had visited the local tower blocks and deck access maisonettes, we had discussed the advantages of tenants groups with anyone who would listen. We had talked of trying to improve the environment, and people taking control of their own lives. After much further work, two struggling little groups got started, mostly focussed on suing the Council for compensation for the terrible state of the flats, and the cockroach infestation of the maisonettes. When they found they could not get any money out of the Council, the groups dwindled. These sower's plants definitely withered!

When we visited the worst complex of tower blocks, we met Alan and talked about tenants' groups. With a little help, he campaigned up and down inside the blocks and produced a meeting that had standing room only. We talked about housing improvements. He talked about driving the drug dealers and pimps from the blocks. They all talked about demanding play facilities and a community room. The "4Bs" had taken off. For the next few months, it was marvellous- a grass roots campaign group was working in Radford with minimal support. This sower's seed had certainly produced a good crop!

The day we heard that Alan and the five other management members had been arrested for armed robbery, we were reeling. The tenants' anger at his desertion and betrayal showed what hopes he had raised. Watching the tenants' bewilderment gave me some ideas about the disciples after the crucifixion. There was a lot of feeling about death and total despair.

He had betrayed them, he had tempted petty criminals into major crime, and the "4Bs" owed debts of £2,000.

But then, incredibly, new shoots began starting up. The black members of the group, none of whom were involved with the crime, started to say that despite what he did, Alan had the right ideas. They are still active. They want to challenge big issues. They won't accept being powerless. They are planning a meeting of a new tenant's group. Is this resurrection?

This also made me think of the passage in Luke 9: 49-50:

"Master," said John, "we saw a man driving out demons in your name and we tried to stop him, because he is not one of us." "Do not stop him", Jesus said, "for whoever is not against you is for you."

Can I also believe that Alan's message of re-building the community, and strengthening it to drive out drug dealers and pimps, was also God acting through people, whatever they had done or go on to do?

Police - The Good Samaritan

In the summer of 1991, when the riots were happening on the North Shields housing estate, and disturbances were breaking out elsewhere fanned by the hot weather, the youth club gang were waiting to cross the Ilkeston Road. A new boy in the group gave a two finger sign to a passing police car. The lone driver over-reacted. swerving his car in a U-turn further up the road and racing back down, siren wailing, crossing the traffic lights on red.

The policeman practically lifted the boy off the ground, wielded a totally illegal whip and loudly threatened him. Fortunately, the boy did not hit him. Fortunately, the other boys did not "defend" him. The incident finished because another police car drew up, obviously worried that the policeman might be in danger. Both got back into their cars and drove off.

When the boy's mother complained to the police, she was amazed to find her story was believed, and a written acknowledgment of fault was forthcoming from the central police station. She was also grateful to find that a youth club volunteer had written to the police in fury at the treatment of a boy she did not even know. The mother had not thought anyone cared about her son except for her, and she thanked her Good Samaritan. But was the Good Samaritan the second policeman who rescued her son?

Injustice can be fought with righteous anger. Defeatism or violent reaction are not the only possible reactions. And Samaritans - policemen? - can be bad and good.

3. Jane and John and Paula and Acts 2

Jane - The Woman Taken

When Jane lied that her caretaking cheque had been stolen, and needed to be replaced, it was very easy to find out that she had cashed it. She is a barely literate local mum who has helped with afterschool clubs and playschemes for several years,. without being paid a penny. For the first time ever, she had been paid for doing something for the group, just before Christmas, when she was always desperate for money.

When a small core of us discussed how we should deal with her dishonesty, we all realised that we had each done much greedier things in our lives. We were just too clever to do anything so naive and transparent. We also knew how much our friendship meant to Jane. We had a real problem about casting the first stone (John 7. 53-8.11). But she had certainly been "taken, in the very act". (John 8.4).

In the end, it was up to me as treasurer to suggest to her privately that she had made a mistake in the confusion of Christmas preparations, and gently to stress that it should not happen again. We agreed that we should look out for paid tasks she could do, and try to find other ways to support her.

John - Nowhere to lay his head

Jesus would have shared a lack of "belonging" with the homeless people who beg in the city and wander round our streets. "Foxes have holes and birds of the air have nests, but the Son of Man has nowhere to lay his head." (Luke 9.58).

Some organisations in Radford try to find accommodation for the homeless in Radford. Macedon, a Christian charity with enormous achievements but a somewhat chequered history, has houses which offer temporary or longer term communal housing for single people.

John initially slept rough, then went to the night shelter and ended up in a Community Housing single bedroom flat. He told of his wilderness experience. Made homeless when his marriage broke down, he had seriously considered suicide. Then he got into various forms of crime, and finally found a sort of fellowship among the city centre drunks. One day, with a bit more will-power than usual, he sought help at All Souls' Church, who introduced him to Second Base housing group, who found him a flat. This son of man had found a place to lay his head - due in large measure to possibilities created by two groups of followers of the first Son of Man.

Paula - and the Great Banquet

Paula is a single parent mother of three mixed-race children. She seems tough and resilient and has found out how to survive on her little money. She applied to a Charitable Trust for money for her children's first ever holiday, but the £100 offered would not go far. At the last minute, she was invited on the local churches' week-long holiday at Kinmel Hall. Her children would be going free, so she could just afford it.

She wasn't impressed by what she knew of Christianity before she went, and she appeared just to have a good time and to be avoiding the religious bits of the week. People chatted with her, played with her children and babysat for her in the evening so that she could go to the pub. On the way home to Radford in the bus, she asked her neighbour why people had been so loving to her. It was a new experience.

When the invited guests rejected the invitation to the great banquet that Jesus talks of in Luke 14. 16-24, the host told his servant, "Go out quickly into the streets and alleys of the town, and bring in the poor, the crippled, the blind and the lame." For Paula, the best of the Great Banquet was not the food but the friendship.

Community House - and Acts 2

No.33 is the terraced house on Radford Boulevard where I base my work. The Methodist Community House has run for over 15 years, and has always had a policy of sharing food, possessions and household expenses, like the fellowship of believers after the resurrection in Acts 2. 44-46. All costs, including rent and food, are divided proportionately, according to ability to pay. The three residents also worship together, hosting a small house fellowship. The requirement of the residents has always been that they contribute to the life of the local community and a local church, whether they are working or unemployed.

House members come not as middle class "experts" from outside to do good to inner city people, but as the accidentally put together base group for a Christian community which can act as leaven for a wider community.

"The Kingdom of Heaven is like yeast that a woman took and mixed into a large amount of flour until it worked all through the dough." (Matthew 13.33).

Recently, two of the residents have come from households and neighbourhoods quite as poor as this one in Radford, and this seems to have helped the household be more a part of the neighbourhood.

****

These stories from my own area suggest the way in which in very small ways the Gospels are being acted out today. Such stories make the contemporary Good News in Britain. A vital part of any such "Good News" has to be that Jesus seems to have rejoiced to act in them and to tell them to others. A contemporary Gospel Christianity - and an Urban Theology - must surely take account of this.

Books referred to:

John Vincent ed., Good News in Britain (Urban Theology Unit: 1994)

Margaret Walsh

STILL HOPING!

1. Learning from the Poor

"The preaching of the gospel to the people of our times, full as they
are of hope but harassed by fear and anxiety, must undoubtedly be
regarded as a duty...."

EVANGELII NUNTIANDI (1975)

It later goes on to stress the importance of our task quoting from the
Prophet Isaiah: "The Spirit of the Lord is upon me because he has anointed
me; he has sent me to preach the Good News from city to city and especially
to the poor...." It adds: "the poor, who are often better disposed to receive
it..." It goes on to say that this mission "must always take the human person
as its starting point", coming back to the interrelationship between persons
and their relationship with God. In paragraph 21, we read:

"This proclamation must be made above all else by witness. We
envisage, therefore, a Christian or a group of Christians as people
who, in the midst of the community in which they live, will show that
they are capable of understanding and accepting others and of co-
operating with all those who are seeking to protect what is noble and
good. We envisage them radiating simply and spontaneously their
faith in values which transcend common values and their hope in
things which are not seen and of which even the boldest minds
cannot form an image."

Signs of the Times. In order to understand and accept others and to
protect what is noble and good, we must be able to continually read the signs
of the times. To do this, we seek the living Christ in our society today by

Margaret Walsh is a Sister of the Infant Jesus, and pioneered and led the
Hope Community in Heath Town, Wolverhampton, whose story she tells in
Here's Hoping, published by UTU. In autumn 1996 she went to India and
has now returned to work on ministry issues.

listening to the hopes and fears of its people. In a society which values individualism, competition and private enterprise, loneliness and isolation are the lot for a growing number of people. Many are lost in a wilderness of apathy and despair. The experience of powerlessness is one of the most common features of life, especially for those who are excluded by those who hold the power. Their lives are spent in a market place existence where their only value is that of consumers. In the past decade there has been a huge transfer of power to unaccountable quangos. In our parliamentary democracy, the cabinet seems to hold most of the decision making cards and these they deal out to those who control the market. Community seems to be the most abused adjective when labelling social and economic policy - at a time when the break down of the family - the basic cell of community - is the experience of families right across society.

In a spirit of prayer and in the contemplation of this reality we come before our Triune God who is our inspiration and guide in reclaiming the values of his kingdom in this country. In a society that exalts the individual over the community this God provides both a challenge and a hope of a new civic society where the individual can realise his true value ie. made in the image and likeness of his creator God through his relationship with others.

Priority to the Poor - 'Staying in the City'. It is very clear from the gospel story that God gave a special place to the most excluded folk. He seeks out the companionship of the outcasts, the sinners, the poor and the broken. They respond to his call because they know their need for him and the hope, freedom and healing that he brings and in the light of this love they begin to realise their own dignity and worth. In Luke 4: 16-21 he inaugurates his Kingdom in terms of Jubilee, where slaves are set free, land and homes are restored and debts are cancelled. He ushers in a Kingdom identified with those normally excluded, the poor, the captive, the downtrodden. His temptations in the wilderness reveal graphically his choice of the powerless and his rejection of power, status and influence (Lk.4:1-14). Jesus turns upside down so many values of our world, where the powerless are the most important, where the 'downwardly-mobile' are the ones on the way to the Kingdom, where the poorest hold pride of place. In his Kingdom the powerful find new life in the way they deal with the poor and the broken; Zaccheus finds his salvation when he answers the call of Jesus and restores justice to the poor. In the Magnificat (Luke 1:46-55), we see that the Kingdom of God is more than the confrontation of individuals but also challenges the structures of society. Again, it is an upturning of the status quo as God takes the side of the poor and hungry against the rich and comfortable.

We find numerous references to the crowds who followed him. They were not a homogenous group and included rich and poor but it is significant that the majority were of the harassed and dejected type. It was no accident that it was lowly shepherds who rejoiced at his birth. Two criminals shared his experience of crucifixion, one he invited to accompany him to paradise. The person who recognised the risen Christ and who was entrusted with the mission of making this known, was Mary Magdalen.

For me, it is such a privilege to find this same Jesus among the poor in Wolverhampton. To be honest, I often feel that I have only begun to understand the Jesus of the gospels in the last few years. It is certainly the most formative experience I have had. Living among the poor, I can see and hear those who followed Jesus in a very real way as I contemplate these gospel scenes. Jesus did not associate with the poor because of their virtue but because of their suffering and their powerlessness and also because of their simple, childlike faith and trust. I am always struck by their humility and also by their desperation when they come forward in public to lay their wretchedness and sin at his feet. I suppose too that those who have so little in terms of status and material possessions are more free to reach out and experience the riches of Christ.

It was to people with this openness and receptivity, the poor of His day to whom Jesus said: How blessed are you who are poor: the Kingdom of God is yours. His Beatitudes of the Kingdom represent the reverse of accepted standards and priorities. They are a challenge to those who make material possessions and status their god. The values of the Kingdom are different and stress love, peace-making, compassion. He goes on to challenge those who are listening to love their enemies, to do good and bless those who hated and cursed them and he reminded them of what their attitude should in the doing of good deeds, when fasting, and in prayer. He sternly warns them that not only should they listen to his words but put them into practice by the way they live and relate to others. He also tells them that he has not come to abolish the Law but to fulfil it. He certainly wasn't offering them a soft option.

2. The Ministry of the Poor to Us

To really take the gospel message seriously, the poor must be helped to recognise their worth and dignity, surrender their apathy, be united among themselves and reach out to their brothers and sisters across the many

it. The temptation to hopelessness and despair is very real for us. When we began to recognise this real danger of losing hope, we decided to call ourselves "The Hope Community" as a reminder of our task to stand ready to explain the hope that is in us (Peter 3:15).

Solidarity. Before we went to live in Heath Town, part of our impossible dream was to go there and 'identify with the people'. We soon learned that to attempt to do this is seen as phoney by the people and only serves to damage any credibility we might have. We have voluntarily chosen the poverty of Heath Town; we are there by choice and we stay there by choice. However, we believe that we can be in solidarity with the people....when we listen to the drills and the diggers, when we wait for broken down lifts, as we wade through the flooded walkways, as we begin to cough and wheeze like most other people. We can live that solidarity all the better when we are more authentic ourselves and ready to make answer for the 'hope that is in us', though we may need a lot of reprogramming in order to be our true selves in a place like Heath Town. Living as tenants on the estate has involved all of us in a reconditioning process.

As Sisters, we are an enigma to the people. Their ideas of nuns have been shaped by films like the 'Nun's Story', that is before they saw the 'Brides of Christ' or 'Sister Act'. Now they are more confused than ever. We are often introduced by them as 'not proper nuns but real people'. This is often followed by questions about us not having partners or children. Our celibacy and our living in community is what seems to fascinate the people and is often the starting point to very deep discussions on the meaning of life, death, God etc. Anyone who joins the community, be they young people looking for a year's experience or church students on placement, are faced with many searching questions about why they are doing what they are doing. We have found that the best way to interview prospective candidates is to let them loose with the locals for a while. We soon discover their motivation and also their gifts for this kind of placement.

3. Becoming Aliens

For us, living in Heath Town means that we no longer have any particular status or identity. As a teacher I had some idea of what my role was and also how I could set about achieving results. Also, I was brought up to value hard work and to earn status through efficiency, competition, success and material possessions. These tend not to be important to the people on the estate, and so early on, I began to wonder who I was and what

I was supposed to be doing in the inner city. It was an experience of great alienation (though one which I had chosen voluntarily); in other words, I didn't feel at home with myself or in my surroundings. I just didn't belong. I now recognise this experience as immensely valuable. It has caused me to question the whole nature of the Kingdom of God and also gives me the opportunity to be in solidarity with a very alienated people who live on the margins of our society.

In the early days of my alienation, I spent a lot of time sighing for the fleshpots of home, and often wondered if I had made a mistake in my journey. On March 17th, I sang the 'Hail Glorious St Patrick' as never before, particularly the last verse: "Thy people now exiles on many a shore". Also, a phrase from the 'Hail Holy Queen' began to take on a new significance: "To thee we do fly, poor banished children of Eve...after this our exile, show unto us the blessed fruit of your womb, Jesus." One day, while listening to the radio, I heard a song I used to know and it gave me plenty of food for reflection: "This world is not my home, I am just passing through. My treasures are laid up some way beyond the blue. The angels beckon me from heaven's open door, no I can't make my home in this world any more." I didn't have a death wish but what the novice mistress used to tell us suddenly made sense: "You must be in the world but not of it."

From then on, many ideas about life and religion began to come together for me. St Paul tells the Ephesians (2:19) that they are no longer aliens and foreign visitors but part of God's household. As Christians, we are often described as a pilgrim people who haven't got a lasting city on earth but we look for the city that is to come. Jesus reminds his followers that "the Son of God had nowhere to lay his head." (Matt. 8:18). As his followers we cannot expect any greater security, yet he promises us life to the full.

Now I am fully convinced that to be aliens is the nature of our Christian calling. If we are too 'at home' and comfortable in what this world has to offer, then I think we must begin to question whether we are in the Kingdom of God. I believe that we should be challenge to the world of comfort and materialism by our lifestyle and values which will be different from the norm. As it says in Evangelii Nuntiandi:

"We should arouse a spirit of enquiry in those who see our way of life. Witness of this kind constitutes in itself a proclamation of the good news."

Desert Experience. Some of us have the privilege of knowing the benefits of a retreat or a desert experience in order to take stock of our lives. I would strongly recommend the inner city for this and indeed we have arranged inner city retreats at our place for a number of people during the years. This is not a commercial because, at the moment, we have neither the time nor the personnel to develop this aspect of our mission. In the inner city, we can soon find ourselves unmasking some of the demons which may be leading us astray in today's world and may begin to ask ourselves deeper questions about who our God is and what do we mean when we pray 'Thy Kingdom come.' It can create the space for us to stand back from our background, our customs and our institutions and critically evaluate them. I read somewhere that we need a healthy dialectic between the margins and the structures. When the structures become increasingly hierarchical, there is a corresponding resistance to what is perceived as a threat from the margins.

In the Scriptures, the wilderness is the place where individuals and groups come face to face with God and come to know the nature of his call to them and his love for them. Yahweh takes on the cause of Hosea who is at his wits end with his unfaithful wife and promises: "I am going to seduce her and lead her into the desert and speak to her heart. There I shall give her back her vineyards and make the Vale of Achor a gateway of hope. There she will respond as when she was young, as on the day when she came up from Egypt."(Hosea 2:16-19) In the Book of Kings, we meet the prophet Elijah fleeing from the wrath of Ahab and Jezabel and spending forty days in the desert. It was there that he encountered God in the gentle breeze and did not find him in the hurricane, earthquake or fire (1 Kings 19:1-18). Moses decision to be in solidarity with his own people, the Israelites, meant a radical departure from the regime of the pharaoh to a new social order. This was made known to him in the wilderness. It was in the wilderness that John the Baptist prepared the way for Jesus and where Jesus prepared for his own ministry.

5. Agenda

We had no particular plans for what we might do when we went to live on the estate. Our conviction was that it is more important to listen to and try to see reality through others eyes and respond with them in the light of the Gospel. We knew that we had a lot to learn from the people. All of that may sound fine in theory, but when you get up in the morning and have no idea of how to spend your day, it can be a little unnerving. I soon found that

I had lost some of the patience and capacity to wait and to sit around with nothing to do. It is so much easier to do things for people than to be with them! Quick, push-button results are so much more the norm today that it is difficult to go without and wait. Now, I happily wander around the balconies, 'loitering with intent', and looking for God and the signs of the Kingdom in unexpected places and people. God definitely has a sense of humour!

Promoting Justice. Before I went to live and work among the people of Heath Town, I didn't really understand the nature of poverty in Britain. I was very involved in a local Justice and Peace group in Crewe, and had no difficulty in understanding Third World poverty and the need to do something about it. My mother used to stress that charity should begin at home so I naturally began to tune into the poor in inner city Britain and raised questions about our responsibility towards them. I had no difficulty in understanding the attitudes of many of my friends: "Our poor have no reason to be hungry or deprived. It is their own fault. Their circumstances are often of their own making. They are feckless and work shy." Still, I knew that there must be more to it than this and I was not willing to go along with these dismissive attitudes. Yet I knew that I needed the concrete experience to really understand.

As Christians and as Church, we know we must have a preferential option for the poor, but this does not mean that we all should work in inner city areas. Our calling within the Kingdom may well be different. Wherever we are, we know that as followers of Christ, we must be actively involved in the promotion of justice and live our calling to make this preferential option for the poor. In many ways, it is easy for those of us who live on the margins and have the concrete reality on our own doorstep - but for the most part we are not in positions to influence any great changes to unjust structures. The system is far too complex for us and we find ourselves standing silent and powerless before it as Jesus did during his trial. We could say a lot here about economic policies that have focussed on the individual, of market forces, competition and consumerism, but let me just say that I fail to be convinced by the 'cascading wealth' theory and smiled when I read one commentator describe it as like a cold shower as far as the poor are concerned.

Community Organising. I have recently found new hope in what 'Broad Based Community Organising' has to offer and am excited about this initiative in the Black Country, called "Citizens". It is based on the philosophy and work of the late Saul Alinsky, who began the organisation in

Chicago about 50 years ago. It invites us to work together in the promotion of true democracy and liberation for all. It means that we have to look beyond our own patch and join other faith communities and together work for a more just society. More importantly, it offers opportunities to people, especially those at the bottom, to exercise their power and their right as citizens.

Reality Through the Eyes of the Poor. By seeing reality through the eyes of the poor, you become more aware of the larger socio-political world. They carry in their brokenness the reality that things are getting worse. People without hope reveal the oversights of the politicians. For example, generally speaking, the people on the estate do not enjoy good physical or mental health. Medical provision is far from adequate and they cannot afford balanced diets, few will have any regular intake of fresh fruit or vegetables, and they seem to be constantly coughing and sneezing and having some virus or other. Holidays away from the estate are the privilege of the very few. Care in the Community sounds great but what is actually happening to those who have left institutional care and those on hospital waiting lists, is a scandal.

Patronising Attitudes. Life is extremely grim for many and they have little hope for a better tomorrow. Our growing dilemma is how not to be patronising when our friends are forced to come and beg for material help. This kind of giving can seriously inhibit the building of community and it also serves to condone a fundamentally unjust system. However, to feed the hungry, and clothe the naked is a clear gospel imperative; hence our dilemma. When you have food and money, it is easy enough to give people what they are asking for and then send them on their way, all can be done in less than ten minutes. I find that it can be much more demanding in a busy day, to sit with the person and give time to unravelling their story in an attempt to discover the root cause of their cold and hunger.

For me, it is a question of how I choose to spend my time - Jesus clearly chose to 'waste time' and to put aside his plans in order to listen to those whom he met on his way - a point well illustrated in his parable of the Good Samaritan, and in the story of the Woman at the Well. The Good Samaritan had not sought the needy traveller but found him on his own journey. The others, keeping to their own agenda, walked on. He was able to help because he was willing to abandon his own road and move into the path of the one who was suffering.

Many church leaders often feel frustrated by the demands of parish commitments and the expectations of the 'church attenders' - often a relatively small percentage of the whole community. No doubt much of it is in terms of providing the Sacraments and getting the lapsed back to church. I sometimes wonder if there is too much of a focus on liturgy and church maintenance and too little on the needs of the whole community.

6. A Way of Life

Prayer, Community and Common Vision. Living and working in the inner city is a way of life that can stretch one to the limits. Sometimes we can only keep going by a deep faith and trust that God is with us. We also have a greater appreciation of the need for love and support within the community and from a wider Hope Community Network. We also know how vitally important it is to have a common vision. We spend a lot of time in community, sharing our meetings with God in our daily lives and also planning ahead and evaluating tasks undertaken. It is an evolving mission and community, chiefly because we are open to conversion by the poor. It is sometimes rewarding, but most of the time we just have to live in an attitude of hope and trust because we do not know how things will turn out.

Local Liturgy and Prayer. Most people on our estate find the official Church irrelevant to their lives. In the past ten years, I have attended three weddings and about three baptisms. The usual reason people give for not availing of the sacraments is that they cannot afford them! Actually, it is not so much the Church they cannot afford, but the party afterwards! We have, however, attended countless funerals. When somebody dies, we are often called upon to assist with funeral arrangements which usually take place at the Crematorium. These can be soul-destroying experiences, especially when the leader of the service has no knowledge of the person who has died or the bereaved family. The ceremony is often over in about 15 minutes. For those who have the body taken to church, there can be a lot of anxiety about how to behave in a church setting because this is often very foreign territory for non-church attenders. Some of the reasons people give for not finding the Church relevant to their lives, are that the Church is too posh and middle class, and they do not understand its language or ritual. But the people really desire opportunities to worship God together. We believe that it is more important to find ways to relate this desire to their own concrete experience, so we have developed a local liturgy and our hope is that we are bridging gaps between the official church and the experience of a very church-alienated people.

Wasting our Time. Some of our church friends still say that we are wasting our time and that we could better use our gifts and training in the more traditional forms of evangelisation. In discussing the issue, I have found negative attitudes towards those on the margins. Some will deny the reality of poverty in Britain, and point to the deserving poor in the Third World, others will point fingers at those who plead poverty as an excuse for not getting on with a day's work.

We are convinced that Heath Town is where God wants us to find Him and His Kingdom. Despite a lot of confusion and doubt, we know that we can continue to give witness to Christian community and to the hope that is in us. Perhaps it is far better and more creative not to have the answers but to keep going forward with hope in our hearts and to explicitly proclaim the Good News when people are ready to hear it.

It would be a mistake to believe that we already know the full message contained in the 'Good News'. So an attitude of being open to discover more of that truth by which we can become free is essential. If this is to be a journey of conversion, then our companions on the road are our friends and neighbours, especially those who are willing to see their reality in the light of God's world and to recognise Him as He walks along with us (Luke 24:15). We know that the more we deepen our understanding of the Kingdom of God, the more effective will be our attempts to work for a social order which will incarnate its reality.

Proclaiming the Gospel. To conclude, I would like to quote once again from Evangelii Nuntiandi:

> ".....witness, no matter how excellent, will ultimately prove ineffective unless its meaning is clarified and corroborated - what St Peter called accounting for the hope that is in you."

The meaning of a person's witness will be clarified by preaching, clearly and unambiguously, the Lord Jesus. The good news proclaimed by witness of life sooner or later has to be proclaimed by the word of life. There is no true evangelisation if the name, the teaching, the life, the promises, the kingdom and the mystery of Jesus of Nazareth, the Son of God, are not proclaimed.

Inderjit Bhogal

GRIEVING IN A MULTI-FAITH SOCIETY

The Sheffield Bereavement Forum had arranged a Study Day on "Religious and Cultural Aspects of Death, Grief and Mourning". The aims of the day were stated as:

- to create an environment where we can explore general principles, the present situation in Britain regarding multi-cultural issues and the importance of taking other cultures seriously.
- to enlarge on the bereavement process and loss of identity in a multi-cultural society.
- to offer opportunities to explore particular faith and cultural issues in small group workshops.

I had been asked to give the keynote address. What follows is the address as I gave it.

****

I will focus on our two main objectives by spelling out, firstly, the fact of plurality and the need to consider all issues from this perspective; and secondly, the universality of the experiences of loss and grief, and the need to help people move towards adjustment and new meanings. I will speak about our plural society, which can be seen as a bane or a blessing; I will speak about the universality and diversity of bereavement, grief and mourning. I want to acknowledge the insights of my colleague, Dr Emmanuel Larty, who comes from Ghana, and who is Professor of Pastoral

---

Inderjit Bhogal is a Methodist Minister in the Sheffield Inner City Ecumenical Mission. He was Director of Studies at UTU 1994-97 and is now Director.

Studies at Birmingham University. His Doctoral Thesis entitled: "Pastoral Counselling in Inter-Cultural Perspective" was published in 1987 and I have gained much from his work for this paper.

1. Plural Society: Bane or Blessing?

Listen to stories of some recent experiences of mine:

1) It was a Monday morning (14th Oct. 96), my day off. I was having a lovely warm soak in the bath at about 9.30am, listening to the Radio Sheffield 'phone-in with Roney Robinson. A number of people rang in to express their concern that families had had to keep an overnight vigil at gravesides at Shiregreen Cemetery. That is the cemetery near Wincobank Chapel where I am Minister. I decided to get out, get dressed, Dog-collar included, and go to join the vigil. When I arrived at about 10.00am, I headed towards a group of people in one part of the cemetery. People were looking a little anxious as this Asian man, dressed as a Church Minister, came towards them. The group, 50 or so women, men and children, burst out into spontaneous applause: "Thank you for coming and joining us," they said. Having gone to stand with them a few minutes, I ended up getting really involved, and not returning home till nearly 4.00pm. I joined 4 women from the group, at their request, to meet local Councillors to find a way ahead. The situation was that the families at the cemetery were protesting at the local Council's request that they should remove the small gardens that had been planted around the grave stones. Gravesides are emotional places, and the feelings at this occasion were expressed by someone like this: "If the Council removes the gardens, we will want to remove the remains of our loved ones."

The families, mostly women, at the gravesides, would not describe themselves as religious, though they used a lot of religious language in conversation and referred a great deal to "Him up there who is looking after us." To me, they were like the women who waited and watched at Jesus Christ's side at Golgotha Hill, and who came to visit the tomb where he had been laid to rest. The little gardens they had created by the gravestone of their loved ones are very beautiful, and I have defended their actions as part of the process of grief, and coming to terms with loss.

2) A man of Muslim faith walked into my office on one occasion, and asked me to pray with him. "I have just heard from Pakistan that my mother has died a few minutes ago. Will you please stop, and pray?" That is just

what we did. The other office staff joined us too. It was a remarkable moment in which death united people of different faiths in prayer. No-one asked the theologically vexed question: "Can we pray together as people of different faiths?" I have been through an experience not unlike that of my Muslim brother. My father died in India during a visit, while the rest of the family were here in Britain. It is an experience that is common to many of us who have members of family in other parts of the world. The other night, when I rang a Methodist Minister, she told me how glad she was to receive the phone call. It was the day of her sister's funeral in Nigeria: "I couldn't go....It was better for me to send money to cover the funeral costs rather than buy air-tickets...It was one thing or the other....it's not an easy choice, and it is painful," she said.

3) A family of Bangladeshi background is known to me. They live in Britain, all of them - except one son who is in Bangladesh. He and the rest of the family long for him to be here. Immigration bureaucracy and procedures are keeping the family separated. Immigration officials refuse to accept that he is genuinely the son of the couple concerned. The suffering and heartbreak of the family is extreme. In an interview with the BBC, the son, speaking from Bangladesh cries in agony and hopes that he will get to see his parents before they die: "If I have to come through fire to see you, I would do so," he says to his mother. Numerous similar stories could be told of similar loss and grief. Equally, stories could be told of people, Asylum seekers, Refugees and others, who have come to Britain from other countries, whose sense of disorientation, dislocation and alienation (if I may use that term in this context) can only be explained in terms of loss and grief.

4) A church at the heart of Birmingham's multi-faith, multi-cultural setting was struggling with me over the whole question of what it means to be Christian in that neighbourhood. At one stage in our discussion, people were sharing some of their anxieties and fears. Some of the older white members who had lived in the area for many years and had witnessed a change of neighbours, described their attitudes with such words and terms as: "I feel threatened by their presence", or "I feel British culture is being eroded". The feelings of change, loss and threat were specifically to do with the numbers of neighbours of other cultures and colours, and the changes in the neighbouring streets.

I asked one person what was meant by the words "British culture is being eroded". The reply was simple and clear:

"I used to be able to go to our corner shop and get what I needed without difficulty. The shop sold what I needed. The shopkeeper spoke English. Now I am lucky to get what I need because they sell mostly continental goods, and I find it difficult to communicate in English. That's what I mean when I say that our British culture is being eroded. It's not how it used to be."

There were others in the meeting who delighted in the changes, and the diversity of cultures in their midst.

I have selected just a few stories to illustrate diversity and plurality in broad terms. I have opted to share stories rather than to bombard you with facts and figures. The stories give a flavour of the multi-faith, multi-cultural nature of British society today. We are Bahais, Buddhists, Christians, Hindus, Jains, Jews, Muslims, Parsis, Sikhs. We are Christians of many national and denominational backgrounds. All faiths have different perspectives. And there are those who are of other ideologies such as Humanism and Atheism.

Such pluralism is not a new phenomenon. What is new is the size of some communities such as the Black and Asian communities who are part of British society. The growing confidence and power of the Black and Asian communities is another new factor and has been demonstrated in the last 20 or so years. This can be seen, for example, in the challenges to the increasingly tighter Immigration and Asylum laws and procedures.

Many anti-deportation campaigns and sanctuaries to protect lives and family unity have been successful and have gone some way to making Government publicly accountable on immigration matters. People of different faiths have participated strongly in Education and debates on Education, particularly Religious Education and Assemblies; Black and Asian Communities are generating wealth and employment in the country; while white majority churches have been leaving city centres and the inner city Black majority churches and worshipping communities of other faiths are moving in, bringing tremendous depths of spirituality to those areas; many people of black and Asian backgrounds have played, and are playing, increasingly important roles in Health issues and Institutions. It seems to me that at every level of society Black and Asian Communities are making their presence felt as they continue their struggles for justice and equal opportunities.

This is an important feature of British society today. People of many religious and national backgrounds have made their homes here. Many of us were born here. Many of us have lived here longer than anywhere else.

This is the context in which we meet. This is the plural perspective from which we must consider all issues in Britain, be they related to Health, or Education, or Law, or Theology, or Housing, or Social Work or whatever. It is a context and a perspective that we must not ignore. It feels very strange to be stating a blatantly obvious fact .... but it is so easy always to assume a white British norm, or a white British Christian norm, or even perhaps a white English norm! It is this plural context which is the delight and great dream of some people, but the despair and nightmare of others.

The Parable of Pitsmoor

On week day mornings during school term, I like to walk with our two children, Liamarjit aged 8 and Anjuli aged 6, to school. At about 8.45am the local streets are crowded with other parents, guardians and children. We reflect the community. We are black, Asian, white, young, middle aged, old. At one point on the journey, many of us have to cross a busy through road, Barnsley Road. At 8.45am, the cars and buses and trucks are bumper to bumper both ways. Cyclists who brave the road wear masks to cope with all the fumes. A lollipop lady assists those who wish to cross the road.

As we wait at the pelican crossing, I look round and feel a thrill at the multi-cultural, multi-coloured, multi-religious group of women, men, boys and girls around me. In the midst of all the local concerns related to the many poor, the many religions, the many trees; in the midst of all the struggle in life we represent, we are a sign of the Kingdom of God which Jesus said is "in the midst of you." And I rejoice and give thanks to God.

As I look around, I see also the faces of people looking out of buses and cars at us. Sometimes as they speed on, people turn their faces in the vehicles to look at us. But the looks are depressing. The faces show a sense of sheer resentment - the faces say something like: "I used to live there. Pitsmoor was a good place. Now its over-ridden by all these 'foreigners'."

And they pass through. That's all they do now....pass through - to town, to work, to homes elsewhere. They do not share my sense of delight at what I see. They only seem to deplore what they see. I want more people to rejoice with me, to see in the city signs of the New Jerusalem, the Kingdom of God.

2. Pluralism: Loss and Gain

I would like to share some reflections in relation to those who despair over the multi-cultural, multi-faith Britain. It is quite possible and permissible to apply the research and insights into loss and change (Marris 1974) to all kinds of situations where the pattern of life is disrupted. It is a normal human reaction to hold on to what is secure, predictable and familiar. When this is challenged, especially by factors which are uncontrollable, by an individual or a community, or perhaps even a nation, there is not only a sense of threat, but grief also for what is lost, a desire to restore what is lost, as well as a will, perhaps, to adapt to change in the future.

It could be argued therefore that many white British citizens, including many white Christians among them, do regard the presence of significant numbers of people of different faiths, in terms of the loss of Britain and British Society and Cultures as they knew these in the past (pre-1945). It could be said also that many of them show little willingness, or show an inability, to adapt to this change in the future.

We cannot ignore the feelings of those who resent the plural, multi-cultural, multi-religious, multi-faith Britain. My own conviction is that this resentment, which can find expression in racist verbal or physical violence, is a manifestation of grief over what is perceived to be a loss. This sense of loss is perhaps a deepening one and may be one of the reasons to account for increasing levels of anger and racism that leads to something like 400 racist attacks a day in Britain, and others throughout Europe.

At issue is the question of British identity, the loss of identity, the change of identity and nationality. What is it to be British? The answer of some people is: "Not black" (cf Gilroy's book There Ain't No Black in the Union Jack.) The fears of people on which so much of the debate on national identity seems to feed is summed up for me in the words of the person from Birmingham whom I quoted earlier. The person feared the "erosion of British culture" with the presence of Black and Asian people in Britain. Some of the reliable and familiar frameworks have been lost for such people. The person in question was at least working with me to seek some hope for the future, but was mourning the loss of the street atmosphere that was once familiar.

Research and insight suggest that change not only involves an element of loss, but also an element of gain, and that change can more easily be accommodated when persons perceive that there is more to gain than to lose. There are people of all shades of colour in Britain who perceive our significantly plural society and context as a gain and are responding positively to it. There are white people who perceive a greater sense of loss and do therefore find it difficult to accept the change. The issues raised by such a sense of grief and loss do need to be addressed. It is important to recognise and to give proper respect to all cultures. I am left wondering, though, how long it will take for the unacceptance of and anger aroused by the changes to move on towards acceptance and adaptation. Apparently the Hutus have been in the area now called Zaire for around four centuries. The hostilities aroused by tribal attitudes linger on to this day. Black people have been in the UK for at least 2000 years - and we are still wrestling with the issues and hostilities aroused. It would be easy to give up in despair in the light of these facts, but they do suggest that there are long term and short term strategies required. In the short term, the immediate task is to help people to see the plural, multi-cultural, multi-faith Britain in terms of change and gain, to help them to be open to learning and growing in their new environment .. and this is a pastoral task. We need practitioners and pastoral carers who can be visionary and forward looking, and who can help people to see that Britain is irretrievably multi-faith and multi-cultural, and not resent this fact but, in the words of the British Council of Churches, first declared in 1977, to see:

"the presence in Britain of significant numbers of people of faiths other than Christian to be within God's gracious purposes".

There are people who "lament and despair" the fact of plural Britain. The despair is not unlike the despair of bereavement. The concerns of those who feel "British Culture" is being eroded do need attention too. The sense of loss and bereavement needs to be recognised as such and to be tackled imaginatively if we are to come to terms adequately with our plural context. If we don't, some hurts will remain unhealed, and there will always be bitter and resentful racists who will carry an unresolved and dangerous anger within them which will have damaging effects upon us all. Such people will not attend training events like this one. Indeed they will not be open to learning and change while some of their deeper needs related to inner fears are not healed.

Similarly there are people of African, Asian or other national origins who live in Britain, some of them refugees, or students, who undergo a real sense of loss regarding their countries and cultures, roots and familiar

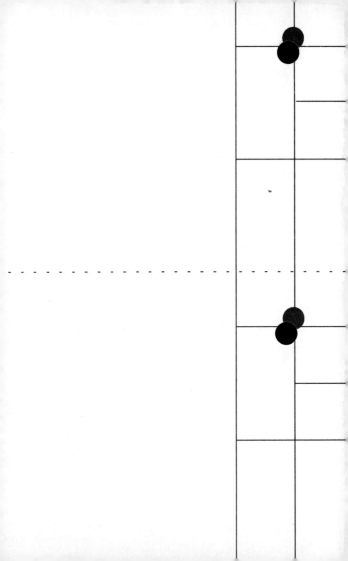

environments. This grief requires attention too. These hurts need attention too.

It is this plural context in which we live and experience all that we do. All the issues raised above are likely to be present at varying degrees and levels in people who are grieving and mourning, people whom we may find ourselves supporting at specific points in their lives. They will have particular needs, but to be relevant and effective, caring professions and persons must pay attention to all that people carry with them in terms of loss and change because they and we live in a diverse, plural context. If we ignore this context and all that it means or represents, it may be damaging and hurtful to people, whether we meet them at points of loss and change, or love and celebration. Where caring professions and people do ignore the plural context, we should attach a "Health Warning" label to them reading: "This could damage your health!"

So a religiously and culturally informed approach to death, grief and mourning would be guided by the facts and realities of our plural context. It would recognise also that plurality means we experience and examine life differently, as white Christians, or black Christians, as Muslims, as Hindus, Jews and so on - all communities that are vast and varied and of international composition - and therefore, we can all arrive at very different understandings and interpretations of our experiences and events.

3. Bereavement, Grief and Mourning: Universality and Diversity

Death: Death is a universal reality, and its rate is constant in all communities, countries and cultures - 100%. Attitudes to death and dying vary enormously though in different cultures and communities.

- Some people are comfortable with the idea of death being "privatised". It has become commonplace in this country that people die in a hospital ward, perhaps often alone, away from the familiar surroundings and dignity of their own home in the midst of their closest family and friends. People hardly see death now, unless of course it is brought to us on the big screen or the TV, or by other forms of media.
- Others are uncomfortable with this development, even with the idea of dying with dignity in a Hospice, and would prefer dying at home - if this privilege could be arranged.
- Yet others are left with the memory or prospect of someone dying far away from family in another country.

- It could be said also, that the greater the advances in science and technology, the longer that people can live now, the further back death can be pushed, the more we seem to fear and deny the reality of death.

Mourning: The attitude to tears and crying vary in all cultures and communities. While some are comfortable with tears and crying, others try to suppress them. Are Hospital staff equipped to cope, and deal respectfully, with wailing from bereaved people, for example, the moment a loved one dies? Is there something about the general reserved attitude to crying in public in white British cultures that puts pressure on people to hold back their tears in public?

Funerals: Is there something about the way crematoriums are organised which prevents an adequate and dignified funeral ceremony? What are the pressures exerted on some cultures, for example, by the 30 minute slots available per ceremony - a time that is reduced to 15-20 minutes when large numbers are present who take time to get in and out of the worship room? The 30 minute slot gives the impression that grief and mourning is a short process, whereas in some cultures the public aspect of grief is an important part of healing and can last for weeks.

Children: A very important issue to consider is children's experience of dying, bereavement, grief and mourning. It would be important to explore, in the workshops, the whole question of how children are involved, or not involved, in bereavement, grief and mourning.

Universality/Diversity: Death may a universal event, and the attitudes to it and traditions surrounding it may be diverse in a multi-cultural, multi-faith setting; But do all people, of whatever culture, gender, geography and so on, go through the same grief process?

Nearly 20 years ago, I read these words of Elizabeth Kubler-Ross:

"If all of us could make a start by contemplating the possibility of our personal death, we may effect many things, most important of all, the welfare of our patients, our families, and finally perhaps, our nation."   (Kubler-Ross, 1970, p16)

These words have guided my approach to death and dying, loss and change, in all their forms. But the last two words, "our nation", took on a new and vital significance for me in the light of my own analysis regarding the sense of loss and despair in so many people in the country. One of the greatest challenges facing us all, this nation, and all the nations at this stage of human history, is the challenge to accommodate more people into our worlds, into our societies, into our tribes. If that means we have to allow closed, monochrome nations and communities to die, then that is part of the challenge. If we can come to terms with our own death, we may be able to help people who experience loss - in personal, family and communal sense, and also in relation to the nation - with all the stages of denial, anger, depression, acceptance, hope and so on.

Fundamental to the kind of healing we are seeking, whether in relation to ourselves, members of our family, or others, or indeed the nation, is a sense of respect and value for ourselves and for others, for our own cultures and for those of others. That respect and value requires of us:

- to meet with those who are different from us for dialogue and to form relationships of mutual trust and respect on the basis of which we can learn from, and about, each other, and work together for the common good;
- to move from white, middle class, male-oriented perspectives of our concerns towards those that encompass larger boundaries of colours, cultures, creeds, genders, geographies and abilities;
- to move from an absolutising and supremacy of white Eurocentric and British Culture towards a pluralism that recognises, respects and values other human cultures as contributing to the wholeness of being human.

Let me conclude with some words from Dr Emmanuel Larty, Professor of Pastoral Studies at Birmingham University:

"Far from replacing Eurocentrism with any other ethnocentrism, what is needed is a wider vision of what it means to be human to which we may each contribute from our diverse historical particularities and cultural heritages."

Bibliography:

Gilroy P.   There ain't no Black in the Union Jack
Kubler-Ross E.   On Death and Dying (Tavistock: 1970)
Larty E.   Pastoral Counselling in Inter-cultural Perspective
        (Peter Land: 1987)
Marris P.   Loss and Change (1974)

Duncan Wilson

GOSPEL VALUES IN INNER CITY CHURCHES

1. An Inner City Scene

Sheffield is a city built on hillsides and in valleys. Streams tumble down unnumbered creases in its landscape from North, West and South to feed the little rivers that swell the mighty Don, snaking out to the East. Each source of water has been a potential power point into which nearly every one of Sheffield's estimated 200 villages has, at some time or other, plugged its local industry. But when steam power came it was the Lower Don Valley, broad with level pastures, that held and fulfilled the promise of major industrial development. Canals served it for transport until and after the railways came, Sheffield being the last major city to be connected to the rail network of the later 19th century. Conveniently, prevailing winds from the South West ensured that the dense and often deadly detritus which the works poured into the atmosphere was blown well away from Betjeman's genteel Broomhill. The "high dormers... stone houses .. and Italianate mansions where laurel and holly co-mingle their greens" were safe from grime but in the huddled dwellings of working families life could be truly grim.

For to the North and South of this wide valley where coal and sweat made iron and steel lived the people who laboured often for a lifetime and one generation after another and not uncommonly for the same "mester". Tight communities of common interest and enterprise clustered together around co-op and ale house, church and chapel. Among these were the

---

Duncan Wilson is a United Reformed Minister, and was from 1989 to 1997 a minister in the Sheffield Inner City Ecumenical Mission, parts of whose story he tells here. He is now minister at Sherwood URC, Nottingham.

inhabitants of Brightside - south facing into the sun through a thick haze - and the folk of Grimesthorpe, Wincobank and Pitsmoor, who laid the foundations of the non-conformist traditions which persist today both in spirit and in style of Christian presence. Day by day and for decades these urban "villages" delivered labour into the valley.

But changes came. First the Great War and then deep industrial unrest. Green fields became housing estates, public services grew and the old workhouses turned into hospitals. Then came war again, dependent upon steel as no war ever before. The Blitz fell upon the city but not upon the valley - the people suffered but industry survived and went on to blossom. Labour then was in short supply and new faces from far away became familiar, there was more new housing stark against the skyline, dwarfing factory and cathedral, and there were more new faces. And then came a word that then and now strikes fear into every worker - rationalisation. In just a few years almost nine out of every ten jobs in the steel industry were gone. The "post industrial age" had begun. Large areas of wasteland and huge derelict sheds lay silent and still. But not for long, as the Sheffield Development Corporation got under way and with its extensive powers, denied to local government, began to plan a "regeneration". It included leisure and sports facilities to international standards, new industrial parts and some housing redevelopment, but, above all, the erection of the Meadowhall Shopping Complex. Steel City was moving into the retail world. Wise heads rightly predicted grave effects for the city centre in terms of lost investment, and a new employment feature - part-timism- proliferated. New and wider arterial roads hastened shoppers and suppliers and after years of upheaval to homes, small businesses and the city centre, Supertram took to the rails, the first completed section leading, of course, to Meadowhall. The era of the labourer was giving way to the day of the consumer.

Now there is clearly immensely more to the story of Sheffield whose history and culture are drawn in much greater depth, richness and diversity. But this is the kind of sketch that local people will draw of the city in which they live and work, at least if they are folk from in and around the Don Valley. It is a large part of the "folk memory" that washes over and around and through the life of individuals, communities and, of course, churches forming an almost unconscious catalogue of reference points whenever issues arise, plans are laid or judgements are formed. It is an intangible but real and sometimes potent influence since it has to do with the formation of the image people have of who they are, where they belong and what they stand for. And it underlines their uniqueness. They are not Bradford, Salford

87

or Teesside and are, therefore, not to be lumped together with them under the description "urban" as though all industrial areas were essentially and predictably the same, common features. Nonetheless they will readily own a kinship with such areas and even speak a common language when describing their life in terms of work (or no work), community (or no community), disruption, poverty, discrimination, powerlessness, political indifference and much more besides. To that extent the insights of people living and working or worshipping and serving in one town or inner city may well connect with those of another and help inform a general picture of the Urban Church and Gospel values.

If that is the case, then rather more of the background needs to be painted in. Picture then a road leading from the city centre of Sheffield. Crowded with buses (of any age and colour since deregulation) it passes due East in line with the River Don and Canal and under the distinctive Wicker Arches of the long defunct railway, which serves the city in place of a medieval gateway. The road splits. On the lower side it leads to the Lower Don Valley, on the north side to Pitsmoor, Firshill, The Northern General Hospital, outlying council housing estates and eventually, after green fields and villages, to Barnsley. But first it negotiates Spital Hill. Here, despite long-standing local authority promises to re-develop it, there remains a depressing shambles of semi-derelict, boarded up and shuttered shells of shops close coupled with bits of 1960s utilitarian office accommodation announcing the discordant tones of inertia, indifference and impending social decay that seem to ring out threateningly over the localities beyond. For even a brief sortie into the council housing estate rising behind Spital Hill will urge the visitor to join the joinery trade. For sheet upon sheet of ply shield either empty or broken-into flats or maisonettes from further pillaging or vandalism.

The sad fact is that many of these dwellings, indeed whole blocks, have only recently been radically refurbished both inside and out and given new roofs and walkways. Phase by phase the whole stock of housing is getting the same treatment but in the meantime the residents are rehoused, block by block, while contractors get to work. The already unstable community is being constantly sent into exile. Many will not be sorry. They will consider it a passport out of the locality they had no desire to live in but no other choice either. Tenancies here last less than four years, so what chance a spirit of community?

Some will say that it has been this way ever since the original "back to backs" came down and the shared yards where everyone knew every else's business were bulldozed away. And this is not sentimentality but a realisation that there are different kinds of poverty. There probably never was a time when material poverty did not stalk these streets and infect the homes from time to time with under-nourishment, illness and indebtedness. Then and now there would be a common sense of powerlessness. But then it was shared and poverty was not uncommon whereas now it is often borne in isolation and poverty appears confined to particular areas. And, to a large extent, hope, individual and communal, has been lost. Personal aspiration and respect are often low. Many have experienced little in their lives to give them the assurance that they are people of some account whom society notices and values. Some give in, a few still climb out and not a few strike out, determined to make their mark - especially the young. Unemployment statistics won't interest them, the reality of worklessness is always with them. And if they are black African Caribbean, even more so.

This is Burngreave. At least that's the name of the electoral ward. But it envelops numerous small localities, distinct in themselves, and with not more than a few hundred inhabitants, all with individual characteristics. Taken overall, 41% of all families are entirely dependent upon benefit, 33% want work and can't find it but that means perhaps 15% in some areas and half the adult population in another. No bald statistics make much sense. Those for housing show that seventy per cent of local housing is in private ownership (though some of it is tenanted or in multiple-occupancy), yet the areas to the North of Spital Hill already described are almost totally occupied by Council Housing or a later generation of housing association development. Another area of large and mainly Victorian houses accompanied by smaller ones in terraced houses the larger part of the local Asian by origin community. The effect is that of a Kaleidoscope where what is the case in one area is coloured differently in another and what is a paramount feature in one is insignificant in another. One further example would be the housing of those with special needs, particularly provision made under Care in the Community. Since existing dwellings or vacant sites can be purchased at comparatively little cost, the whole area, but particularly one part of it, has seen a proliferation of residential provision to the extent that the local community is hard pressed to provide the supportive interest expected of it.

2. Twelve "Signs of Life"

All this appears to present a bleak picture but is not the whole truth. It is true that the communities are under constant and sometimes severe pressure but not true that they lack any resilience or resourcefulness. For a number of small initiatives have been taken by individuals and groups which show the imagination or muscle that can be generated by strength of concern or concerted anger. Thus a group of local residents combining all colours, cultures and religions stood out against the granting of council planning permission for yet another profit motivated hostel. Discovering their common strength of purpose the same group took up the possibility of turning the same premises into a multi cultural centre. Elsewhere people unite to find resources for the development of child care, welfare and recreation. There are many other examples. Apathy does not reign everywhere. Initiatives are on the increase and local churches are involved with them. They include family support and child centred outreach, some in Partnership with NCH Action for Children, some supported by United Reformed Church funding. Some of it breaks new ground and is carried out by members simply walking the streets and meeting local folk and children or leaving their doors open for children to come in and bake, play games or talk. Some of it is a continuation of an unbroken "mission to children" reaching back to the days when James Montgomery wrote words for an opening hymn to celebrate the creation of a "Children's Church" in Upper Wincobank. Here, children in the church still outnumber the "adults" by more than three to one. In the same places a great variety of activities built by and upon elderly folk, proliferate. Community Transport provides the necessary access. Church members are its mainstay not only for management but for fund raising and daily co-ordination. Lunch clubs meet to respond to the needs and cultures of all kinds of local folk, most recently people with learning difficulties. Their annual general meeting to choose officers, approve the finances and plan the next year's outings has to be one of the highlights of the year. This is empowerment and participation at its most natural and therefore, its best. Elsewhere, partnerships have developed providing recycled furniture for recently homeless families starting up home afresh. Conversations between Muslims and Christians slowly generate trust and identify common interest and action. There is the potential for much more and this brief list does nothing to recognise the personal involvement of a great many local "good neighbours" and "Christian activists" who link up with others or go it alone to raise or attend to local awareness of need or opportunity.

And so to the churches themselves - the local places of liberation - invoking issues of style; I name twelve.

a. Indigenous Individualism

The churches now in the area and just beyond it were born at different times and for different reasons. What they have become in the meantime has been formed by a wide range of changes in the city, its industry and local communities. Each one reflects periods of immigration. Labourers came down from Scotland and across from Ireland long before their comrades from Jamaica, Pakistan or the Yemen. Their families soon followed. The desire to preserve their identity and culture was strong, as strong in a Catholic or Presbyterian way as in a Muslim one. Their local input has proved indelible whether upon church or community. It has rendered the churches enlivening. Integration of these cultures would be too great a claim to make and who is to say that that is what should be aimed for? The local alchemy is strengthened rather than weakened by the retention of distinctive characteristics of origin, memory and upbringing. Different voices speaking with the different music and accent placed upon a common language offer something special and precious to the life of the local congregation. And it is more than voices. It is dress and food and home and hospitality as well as forms of greeting and signs of endearment. That which some regard as a source of friction in society, race and colour, in fact greatly enriches both church and neighbourhood.

b. Smallness

So the churches are mixed - and they are also small. Some have less than ten members and make an art form of living precariously on the verge of extinction. The art is to grow new "green", even tender, shoots on the vine as old ones fall away. Some "borrow" fellow travellers for a while, others rely on children to make a congregation of any size but they too are church, they also serve and bless. Other churches maintain what some consider almost the ideal size of company of around thirty folk who intimately know each other's gifts and ways. They may not be strong as financially viable units when it comes to maintaining paid ministers or keeping up with building repairs but in terms of communication, planning and mission, the churches tend to operate almost as extended families. It is possible for them to be inclusive without being constantly introspective. And age is turned to advantage.

c. Churches of Elders

If small, the churches are also dependent upon the older generation. Many commonly judge the vitality, even "success" of the local church by its power to attract the younger generation. Here, however, it is the old who often carry the vision of youth and fulfil Joel's unlikely expectation. It is often they who know that the church is capable of greater effort or generosity, that prayer has no substitute, that God's foolishness shames the wise, that faith means taking risks and that Christians cannot afford to judge by worldly standards. They are elders in more ways than one and as such are indispensable, especially for their example. Many, unhappily perhaps, free or distant from family ties make themselves available in service and pastoral care to an extent which is quite impossible for the busy younger generation. They also bring penetrating wisdom to the councils of the church. Many are the survivors of numerous personal traumas, loss may be a continual ache within them, but, towards the end of life they know and show what it is in human life which has enduring value. In order to survive, small congregations need confidence. Crises are never very far away. But the older generation, far from being thrown from what often feels like riding the roller-coaster of constant uncertainty, know how to remain stable in its twists and turns. For where we are today is not where we may find ourselves tomorrow.

d. Non-Planning

Five year rolling plans are not the prophetic tools of these local churches. That is not to say that there is a lack of vision or a casual approach to planning but that experience has shown up the limitations of identifying specific goals and the fatal error of planning God to the margins - or - simply ignoring God to support our bright ideas. Energy and effort employed with wisdom, love and obedience to what was apparently God's will has often been subverted by the late arrival of some "God send". It has proved infuriatingly unsettling whilst at the same time forcefully reminding us "of our place". It has also been evidence of God's Grace that when we have striven to do our best in adversity, God has yet something better in mind for us. No other interpretation of events has been open to us and there have been many such events.

e. Gospel Opportunism

In one instance, well developed plans for the demolition of a "life expired" church and the purchase of a new site together with the plans for fund raising and the approval of various authorities was well under way when a redundant public house, The Furnival, was offered for sale by auction. It was ideally situated and with some alteration offered accessible and varied accommodation we had not even dreamed of - and at a fraction (so it proved) of the cost of building one. One moment we were still striving to make things move for us (or God, we surmised), the next we had the sense of being caught up in a "movement". All that we had attempted to gain by our own strength and wisdom appeared to pale by comparison with what we encountered as "given".

In another situation the "given" was the totally unexpected offer of a church Elder to set aside her work as a teacher in order to take up, with little assurance of funding, the role of co-ordinating a church's vision of extensive outreach to local children and families. In one moment we were at an impasse having a plan but not means to advance it and an opportunity (a growing number of children in our midst) but no way of claiming it - the next we were given the opening. At other times those twin agents of the Holy Spirit, plain desperation and sheer necessity have driven us to solutions previously ignored or rejected. "Give us today, our bread for today" has been the prayer we often said, not realising what we were asking for or who, indeed, we were asking. Being in many ways uncertain about tomorrow, though not careless about it either, has ceased to be a source of anxiety. We have encountered Grace. So, that even failure may be a sacrament, too.

f. The Value of Failure

In his book, "The Priesthood of the Poor", Andrew Rhodes speaks tellingly of the place of failure, vulnerability and brokenness in the life and self sacrifice of the Christian community. The gaunt and scarred remains of the once wealthy, prestigious and influential monastic community based upon Fountains Abbey form one of his illustrations. He suggests that today's thousands of visitors are more likely to be moved by its stillness, dignity and presence than were ever those who once stood in admiration of its wealth and influence. What was built to the glory of God may, therefore, give greater glory in its brokenness than in its proud success. It is as though the signs of failure themselves communicate the deeper love and purpose of God.

It would be pretentious to draw comparison between such a moving insight and the evidence and experience of our own modest failures. And yet we know that something of what is true about God is communicated by, or through, or despite our limitations and apparent failures. For we often feel exposed. One of our buildings, now demolished, stood as stark and battered against the local concrete landscape as Fountains does against it wooded hillsides. Here no intricate tracery has given way to the assault of some puffed royal vandal bent on making his mark, but plain Victorian sash windows have offered themselves as the target for a younger generation more bored than bad who also needed to show they could leave an impression. The implied rejection, especially in the face of a faltering children and family support project working from the building, is hard to bear. Who knows what message it conveys? Some of the children who inflict this kind of damage and snatch handbags from unwary elders on their way to church can be found later in the same week in junior club apparently happy to accept the company, love and tolerance of the same people whose church they have made the target of their little "intifadas". Some of them may be seen rooting, as casually as they can, through plastic sacks of clothing awaiting a jumble sale. Small hands stuff selected items up oversized jackets - this after all, is the enterprise culture and they have learned already that only number one is going to look after number one. That is, unless by some little miracle they become puzzled by their acceptance among those they have already wronged. Here there are no obvious definitions of what is failure or success. Only love, patient, foolish, exploited and sometimes, angry love, matters. It is the cost of including everyone within the circle of Christ's friendship.

g. A Church at Tables

"For the Church is like a Table"

None of the congregations have set out with theological deliberation to make tables such a significant feature of their life together. Only reflection makes their centrality so clear. The association with meals and celebrations is most obvious, hospitality being a central expression of opening, welcoming, serving, caring, sharing, uniting and enfolding. Without intending it, the agape meal is everywhere. It has formed a focus of church meeting, ecumenical exploration, strategic planning, fund raising and much more. There are parties, celebrations, thanksgivings, Christian (and some non-Christian) festivals, farewells, hellos, achievements not to mention the proliferating lunch clubs. A meeting without a table at the centre or within the circle is almost unknown. The prosaic injunction to all members to "bring and share" carries with it, unintentionally, the very essence of local communion/community. What is brought to the table to share is not always food but prayer and planning or discussion or debate, learning and listening. Here priorities are hammered out, minds get changed, issues are faced and differences are resolved.

"At a 'table that is round'"

The second line of Fred Kaan's hymn is a powerful if simple observation. For it underlines what it means for us to be the Laos. We do actually, habitually, sit in the round and whilst some are acknowledged for the office they hold, their place is "in the round" whilst lines of discussion cross the table.

"To celebrate the healing of all excluded feeling"

The table does, indeed, become the focus of unity where there is regard for everyone and their contribution. Given the ecumenical nature of relationships between both churches and other units, the regular circulation of meetings and gatherings to each location in turn further emphasises the hallowing of every board in every place and affirms the hospitality of every congregation. No one who has read the gospel account of Jesus at table will fail to recognise the role of hospitality in Jesus' relationships with both friends and strangers. The Acts of the Apostles records how the followers of Jesus met to break bread in private houses and shared their meals with "unaffected joy". No local church has sought to deliberately imitate these models, if such they are, and no thoroughgoing theology of hospitality has been worked out. In the main it has been sufficient to know that where welcome and hospitality led, Eucharist was not far behind. And that which serves to bind us in common cause has also come to be realised as a form of mission. In setting out the "style" of outreach from the newly acquired Furnival Pub in the very centre of the area referred to in the introduction, hospitality is seen to offer great promise. It is after all, the mainstay of what the "public house" has been for centuries, complete with "Mine Host". It begs only a little imagination for us to be able to think of a church which advertises "opening hours" but is always open and is never without refreshment and makes visitors guests. For people more familiar with being pushed around or displaced, a centre of unconditional acceptance run as an "open house" may signal the genuine offer of Christian friendship.

h. A Church of Prophecy

We "prophesy at the drop of a hat".

Christians under pressure of living and working in changing or already radically disrupted local communities with, perhaps, slowly declining resources of money and people and exposed to the crime, vandalism and cynicism of resentful local individuals, have had plenty of practice at asking themselves why they remain in being. Well, they are not sheltering from the storm! When Elijah had taken refuge in the cave and watched earthquake and fire pass by he at last came forward, muffled in his cloak to face interrogation from the Lord. "Why are you here?" demanded the sound of silence. "Because of my great zeal for the Lord of Hosts," came the reply. No such timorous or even pretentious response is offered by the councils of the churches. There is no hint either of hollow courage in their insistence that they stay, neither is their vision limited to that of stubborn survival. The explanation lies more in the simple, sturdy, Christian faith of members who have lived and worked long enough in their various localities to know that, however modest the mission, it is an effective co-operation with God for good, however limited their power to liberate change and challenge the status quo. Sometimes it is surprisingly unlimited! So when asked, and they are asked, why they could or would not withdraw, disperse, amalgamate or rationalise, there is no hesitation in drawing attention to their commitment to being the church in the places where they believe Christ also is to be found despite apathy or rejection. They are reinforced in this view by the recollection that they have been this way before. Some very small causes, almost on the verge of extinction with the loss of the last elderly, native membership, have known Easter risings from previously unsighted sources. Elijah's "I, I only, am left" proved to be a miscalculation which God quickly set right. New members, local people, or some borrowed from sister churches have joined the enterprise, quickly got the picture and fanned the dying embers into flame. Thus churches are not described as having a life span contained within birth and death, opening and closing, but as being constantly replenishing and reviving.

i. Risk-Taking

Prophesying, setting out the explanations for even the minor day to day decisions and actions in terms of "God's will" or Christian conviction is more common than folk realise. It constantly rehearses what is believed. Low, even uneconomic charges for the use of church premises by local community groups is a simple illustration. The argument in favour points to the desire to support others whose activities would otherwise cease to function with the consequent loss of precious local gifts and initiative. It also points to the possibility of extending a network of local partnership, of developing relationships, of investing interest in and care for the section of the community being supported. It is seen as affirmative of the good that others do and as an opportunity for encouragement. For the good others do is God's goodness too. Imagination places us, ourselves, in the role of being Christ unto others. So risks are taken, losses are sustained, but not without choice. No one imagines that we can afford to keep on taking foolish risks but, paradoxically, few imagine that we can afford not to. Sacrifice, even modest sacrifice, rarely rationalises in the world's terms but says much about Gospel values. Some translate it as an entrepreneurial approach but they are mostly outsiders.

Prophecy, therefore, is announced by actions and commitments rather than from lips that often have the power to deceive or exaggerate. But prophecy it is and explanations will be supplied on demand - at the drop of a hat - if needs be.

j. Growth from Within

And we grow from our resources.

It has already been said that where we are today is not where we may be tomorrow. It is also true that who people are and what they are able to do or make or give today will not be the same tomorrow. For leadership is a key issue and its development the cause of great encouragement. The need for people to lead frequently calls upon the faith and unclaimed potential of people who have, in previous churches, rarely been called forth from the shadows. Nervous and uncertain in the beginning but affirmed by appreciative congregations, new leaders steadily emerge. Apart from their value to the congregation there is personal growth and fulfilment. It is what Dora Greenwell calls "their hour of life and bloom". It is not a sentimental observation. What she says about "All, all that life hath long repressed" unfolding and "undreading blight or blame" is true. It is not only among the young that it is encountered, in fact it is, if anything, more evident among those who in earlier life "missed their chance" or lived in the shadow cast by brighter lights or were simply led to believe and meekly accepted that they were no great shakes at anything. On this basis churches have proceeded to expect that human resources would be enriched and extended. Furthermore, it encourages the church to look upon itself as a learning place, a trial ground.

In practical terms, it has produced the kind of situation where practically half a small church's membership, meeting a leadership crisis in its children's work, "enrolled" to plan, prepare and train for leadership. Worship, likewise, has fallen to a wide range of lay preachers, elders, stewards and not a few "ordinary" members. Some of the latter have been persuaded to deliver the "one sermon" they had in them and have left indelible memories of their moving testimony. Periodic, short term, learning programmes prepared with and for local members have drawn considerable numbers and primed the interest in both learning and teaching.

And, it should be remembered, there is no better gift to a congregation than the wise "elder" who is an accomplished "talent spotter" for God. Many have first heard the call to ministry in this way.

k. Creative Accounting

And we use (God's?) creative accounting.

Churches do need to be financially viable. In simple terms, bills have to be paid, repairs and renewals have to be carried out and projects supported. To some it may appear that the only way to balance the books is to "cut the garment according to the cloth" - to keep the expenditure side of budget balancing under strict control. But this often seems to go against our grain, our natural inclination. Economic realities cannot be ignored but it is surprising how far they can be stretched and somewhere in memory there is recalled what Jesus managed to achieve with five loaves and two fish. So we often find ourselves with a begging bowl in one hand whilst providing "hand outs" with the other. Some consider it shameless or just economically inconsistent approach to money. In many way, however, it points to the style adopted and in many ways proves to be the only way of "doing" mission. The reality is that local projects and ministries are dependent upon the support of denominational bodies, trusts and agencies prepared to venture their capital. Some of this support is not promised for long and thus there is a constant search for new and willing accomplices. The resort to a local authority that is patently broke and waving its own begging bowl towards the voluntary sector for all kinds of support in areas of social and community work it can hardly sustain, is clearly a waste of time and yet "partnership" is a key word in both their thinking and ours. Small budgets devoted to health and safety, education and crime prevention in particular can be accessed and are. They can at least be used to level other funding or to prime fundraising for modest projects.

There is, of course, the possibility of "realising assets". This is not the selling off of the communion silver but claiming the inherent value of what had come to be regarded as liabilities. The land adjacent to or upon which church buildings have stood is a clear example. Imagination, persistence and the choice of the right moment have claimed these buried treasures for quite major redevelopment projects whose "spin offs" for mission have been considerable. They have also proved to have significant effects on the spirit, morale and cohesion of congregations involved. They merit a story of their own. Land in the inner city usually has little, if any, intrinsic commercial value but does have an attraction to housing associations and other groups keen to develop small schemes in areas of deprivation and often for people with special needs. Thus the local church whilst serving its own need of regeneration may indirectly assist a not dissimilar aim within the secular context. This is truly creative accounting.

1. Generosity

But something has to be added to this. And that is the discovery of generosity in the midst of poverty. Here are reminders of Paul's observations to the Corinthians about the "grace of generosity" shown by the Macedonian churches in their insistence on being included in the collection for starving and captive Christians in Jerusalem. For a rich seam of generosity is to be found among those of very modest means throughout SICEM. It is the source not only of reliable financial support but also the assurance of commitment and a sign of enthusiasm. One church has even tithed its steadily diminishing balances year upon year in a deliberate desire to give support to three or four local, national or international charities. Their Junior Church children even designed, printed and sold their own Christmas cards to the same end. One church member returns to her native Barnsley every year to collect for Oxfam in the streets where she used to live because no one could be found on her departure many years ago to continue her "round". It is important to be creative with money and assets.

3. "Gospel Values"

It is only upon reflection on what has gone before in this chapter that an awareness of Gospel values becomes apparent. It would be misleading to suggest that the churches and projects spoken of have poured over a philosophy or design for being the Church in the inner city before entering upon the various stages of their mission. Action and reflection models are not assiduously pursued and neither are social audits carefully employed - in a formal sense. This may smack of a less than serious or, as some would insist, "professional" approach. But it is neither disregard for well-proven ways of working in and with communities nor a sign of casual irresponsibility. It is rather that Gospel values have simply become so embedded within the culture of the local church that they have seemed to become inseparable from its daily style of living and working. Gospel values will, however, tend to surface on their own account as ideas are tested, when failure or success provoke examination, or the cost of something apparently worthwhile is weighed in the balance. Crises also, both large and small, call for the revisiting of 'Should we still be doing this?' or 'Who do we think we should ask?' questions. Gospel values, therefore, do not go unobserved, but it is through the praxis, the culture and the custom rather than the discipline of strategic planning that they are recognised and affirmed.

And it is also through the form and content of worship. The relatedness of worship to each local situation and the life of each local congregation is an imperative. It is assisted, of course, by the availability of a considerable number of local worship leaders. Beyond this, short term 'series of studies' on subjects related to Lent or comparing five Gospel writers or four prophets are linked with the question 'But what do they say to us today?' So there develops a sense of accountability to what we believe God is saying through Scripture. To some extent this is reinforced by the persistent use of the word and concept of discipleship. This has tended to enhance the sense of each one being called and empowered to offer a personal ministry - to be an active part of the body of Christ. It has also served to underline two important understandings about membership, that members are both followers and learners of Christ. It also helps to break down any exaggerated sense that some are leaders only and some are followers, some teachers and some learners only. It also binds wide age ranges.

Thus the answer to the simple enquiry 'Why are you doing this?' could be a simple as 'It is what Jesus would be doing'. Being aware of the Gospel is as much a gift of the imagination as it is of the intellect. People know enough of their bible to have embraced the 'Word of God' not in a collection of words but in Jesus, the Word of God. When one member calls up their picture or understanding of this person who calls, teaches, touches, heals and sets people on their feet, it is recognised by others. He is given the right to make good, to direct, to guide, to unify and liberate. It has to be his mission or it is none at all.

So, the point has been reached at which it is possible and necessary to add to the 'Gospel styles' of being urban churches, some description of identifiable 'Gospel values' although both are twined together. There is nothing to justify the view that they are not to be observed in other than urban churches. It just so happens that in our urban churches, we find them at work - when we choose to look! Here, the words of John the Baptist's disciples come to mind. As they approached Jesus on their master's behalf, they asked him, 'Are you the one, or do we look for another?' There and then, so the record goes, Jesus healed many who were suffering before delivering the answer, 'Tell John what you have seen and heard; how the blind recover their sight, the lame walk, the lepers are made clean, the deaf hear, the dead are raised to life, the poor are hearing the good news, and happy is the person (he surely stressed that) who does not find me a stumbling block.' Echoes of Jesus preaching his first sermon in Nazareth from the book of the prophet Isaiah are clear. But what if the disciples of John were to approach us, in our place, today? That it seems is the acid test for Gospel values. Because Jesus himself sets out the criteria for being 'God's genuine article' and that surely is what the Church is also supposed to be. 'Are you the ones, or do we look for others?' they might ask.

And perhaps we might turn round and even venture that, yes, the blind do receive their sight again, the lame do walk, the lepers are made clean......and the poor hear good news......look and you will see. It may sound preposterous but, in truth, is the church being the church at all if such things are not witnessed? And so I venture some examples. For wonders do take place and though they may lack the literally astounding directness of those Jesus performed, their effects are much the same. If miracles are not magic but the recreating power of faith then we know that miracles are with us.

For the lame do walk. Arthritis is a commonplace and debilitating disease affecting many of our elderly folk. It would be easy to assume that active membership was not for them and to consign them to the sidelines out of sympathy and concern. But it is not so. All that is possible has been done to ensure that being lame, still they walk, participate and contribute. It has taken many forms. One church in the process of major renovation changed the entrance of its church from one side to the other in order to lead from a new ramped entrance designed within the planning of a small group of new houses within its grounds. Gone was the dark and awkward stepped entrance so long a hindrance to so many. Community transport puts four wheels in the place of legs and many individual hands help the legs of others to bear their weight and maintain their balance. Love does it. And who is Love? In recent times one member was finally restricted almost entirely to her home by two severely arthritic knees. Surgeons offered to operate on both at once. Her family hesitated - she was already over 80 and there was no knowing how stress might affect her tendency to depressive illness. Then with encouragement from her church who could offer no great wisdom, only support and commitment and prayer, she took the first leap. She decided she wanted to be better, to live, not 'wobble through'. Now she walks - 'no sticks either' she would say. Another member knows that her answer is different. Being determined to preach (she is 84) she saves her strength, for standing.

We might add that the deaf hear. One member whose hearing is very restricted and is yet brave enough to demand any preacher to 'speak up', is one of our most skilled counsellors. For while she may hear only with great difficulty, she has trained herself to be a very careful listener. She hears more than most people do of the true joy and turmoil in other lives as she engages in conversation with lonely local folk who find their way into our lunch clubs and other activities. She hears because she cares and respects.

And the dumb speak. Here examples abound. But one of the great gifts of the Holy Spirit was the loosening of tongues and the opening of mouths to the astonishment of hundreds of bystanders. It is one of the gifts which our churches have enjoyed that people have begun to speak, have been liberated to say their piece, to express a view, to say a prayer, to lead a meeting, to knock at the local authority's door, to appeal to those in power, to raise a voice in protest, to become advocates for others, to break the silence on their inner anger or despair. 'Lose your shyness, find you tongue' says Brian Wren's hymn - just so, and with many such little miracles it not only serves the person themselves for growing confidence, but contributes greatly to the local church's store of gifts. And in one particular case, one person who really did come to us practically without speech, at least coherent words, found his tongue on Christmas Eve. One of many local walkers of the streets under the 'Care of the Community', he had offered to read that 'lesson' recalling the breaking of the good news to shepherds in the fields of Bethlehem. Previously, he had made his mark among us by observing and fulfilling little tasks that were telling in their sensitivity and thoughtfulness. Latecomers to worship, neglecting in their haste to pick up a service book, would find one in their hand. He noticed what anyone else seemed to lack. On the night in question no-one was quite sure that he would remember his place and all felt the possibility of embarrassment should he find his task beyond him. But in dim candlelight he addressed the lectern as if a veteran and clearly reading every verse to its end before announcing it out loud, he rendered the proclamation of good news to shepherds with complete coherence in a steady voice and transformed the telling of one of the best known stories, so that it felt like we had never heard it before. No words can describe the sense we had of being in the presence of a special moment and a hidden power. It was simply a gift. And someone said afterwards: 'I hadn't realised he had an Essex accent.'

And do the poor hear good news? The answer must be that, hopefully, they see it, sense it, feel it, meet it, take part in it and find joy in it. All the actions of the local churches must affirm 'good news'. The only regret, perhaps, is that it does not reach nearly so many as they would wish. Any form of communication is being used. Personal forms are preferred because relationship lies at the centre of taking and receiving good news. For some, the simple good news is that they do after all matter to someone. Some are surprised at the time they are given, the interest in their lives, the concern about their troubles. Others are not used to someone else 'putting themselves out' for their sake or their children's. Being noticed, being someone whose views or ideas matter, is a new experience to some folk. In due course, some want to become part of 'what is going on', questions begin to flow and then offers of their own involvement. It is a case of finding the 'touching place' in each person as, perhaps, Jesus found it in Peter.

It comes back to being what Jesus might be, with whom Jesus might meet, in places where Jesus might be present. If the Church is Christ's body, then it must breathe and sigh with his breath and exert its limbs with his energy and his concern, with his alacrity and his response, with his imagination and his love, with his expense and his work with his desire.

Gospel values are, in the end, described by the life of Jesus. They are clarified by his teachings. Gospel values, therefore, are not only affirmed by who we try to be, but what we try to stand for. The two are clearly one in the life of Jesus and so, one would expect, they are in the life of his church. Teachings from the Sermon on the Mount, the implications of parables, the direct conversations of Jesus with his contemporaries are constant reference points as much as the common memory and cultural heritages referred to earlier. Each informs the other to produce a Christian response. In our situation, it is a response to those living in our locality that is appropriate to their experiences, gifts, ideas, needs or whatever. And our locality is inner city. But any response is difficult without relationship and, at that, a relationship of trust or, at least, respect. With a bit of bending, that word 'respect' translates not far short of Agape. It is what counsellors sometimes call 'unconditional positive regard'. If Paul's theology is to be trusted, then the whole story of Christ's coming is a story of the restoration of lost relationship with God and thus, and at the same time, with each other. The greatest restriction in all our work has been the extent to which local churches could form creative relationships with the people in their localities. Community simply does not exist in most places if what community means is some sense of common identity or shared purpose or committed relationships. Therefore, the church has had to content itself with relating to small groups, families or individuals. Fragmentation and estrangement, feelings of being 'ill at ease' where they live, are common experiences. Perhaps the only things that are generally shared by folk living in these localities are a mixture of resentments and frustrations, suspicions and tribulations. Sometimes there has been, however, sufficient anger to unite folk right across racial and religious 'barriers'. Not in our areas but in others, community organising has seized upon these apparently adverse feelings in order to create a concert of protest for positive ends. It does remind us of the Gospel's mission of making good out of evil and thus no situation can be regarded as without hope.

And so, a summary of our 'discoveries' though not exhaustive, might go something like this in relation to our grasp and expression of 'Gospel Values' in the Inner City Church.........

That where Christ and his people are.......
they make clear that everyone is a child of God;
    that those not within the church are not necessarily far from the
    Kingdom of God;
they lay a table where all are welcome, where strangers find a home;
they recognise that everyone has an offering to bring;
they find faith where no-one else looks for it;
they notice people whom others ignore or diminish;
they celebrate the 'greatness of the small';
they give space for everyone to fail, to learn, to grow;
they make mercy and generosity servants of renewal;
they never force an entry into other people's lives;
they warn against making rules more important than relationships;
they show that love finds joy in being spent;
    that being broken or vulnerable also reveals God's presence;
they expect change to be possible for everyone;
they patiently wait to find each person's 'touching place';
    and promise that, wherever Christ is,
    the blind do recover their sight,
    the lame do walk,
    the deaf do hear,
    the dumb do speak,
    the living are brought to life
    and the poor do hear good news.

John Vincent

AN URBAN HEARING FOR THE GOSPEL

1. "Suspicion" in the Inner Cities

"Suspicion" is often the beginning of knowledge and self-knowledge. Liberation Theologians say that when the people of South America start becoming aware of the facts of their existence, they develop a "hermeneutic of suspicion", whereby they sift the things told to them by "authorities" either in state or church.

A "hermeneutic of suspicion" is the best way to describe my own experiences of living with the Gospel in the inner city.

From a personal point of view, I had decided when I took my doctorate in New Testament in 1960, that it was impossible to be teaching or believing in Markan discipleship (the subject of my thesis) without living and practicing it. I had therefore said to myself that I needed to "find a place where Gospel things might happen." Knowing nothing of the Preferential Option for the Poor , or the Hermeneutical Privilege of the Poor, I had instinctively but firmly chosen to minister in housing estates and urban areas - Wythenshawe (1956-62), Rochdale (1962-69) and Sheffield (1970 to date).

Part of this decision was a suspicion of Biblical scholarship that debated and dissected Gospel texts and stories without living them, and of biblical

John Vincent, UTU Director 1969-97, now Director Emeritus and Honorary lecturer in Biblical Studies and Supervisor for MPhil/PhD in Contextual, Urban and Liberation Theologies at Sheffield University.

scholars who made money out of writing and lecturing on events and people in biblical history with which and with whom their own lives and discipleship had not the slightest coherence. (1)

The decision in 1969 to start the Urban Theology Unit was an attempt to bring together my two vocations - the vocation to be a student of discipleship in the Gospel tradition, and the vocation to be an inner city missioner, which to me followed from the first. UTU's first Study House on Abbeyfield Road, opened in 1973, was designed as a place where location, style, colleagues and neighbours would ground theology and discipleship firmly in the realities of a secular, post-Christian urban area of need, alongside tiny congregations of urban disciples, and much larger groups of the deprived in the streets all around.

A few conclusions have come to me simply from living here. The inner city or housing estate disciples of Christ, like all residents there, begin with an innate suspicion of all professionals. The Church ministers are professionals, so they are suspect. They have been educated, so that they know what is the right thing to do, and they know what is the right way to understand Christianity. They are the ones who teach the lay preachers, who generally provide a mix of plain truth and minister-dictated unplain truth. The inner city or housing estate Christians have rarely been asked their opinions on anything, and generally assume that their opinions are thus not worth seeking.

The inner city Christian experiences that the Gospel is heard in a confused way. Mainly it is read and explained by the ministers who have been trained in biblical exegesis. This in itself does not help too much, as there seem to be different "schools", and one interpretation contradicts another. But ministers at least presumably know why they contradict each other.

Occasionally, the simple, down-to-earth stories of the happenings in the days of Jesus actually get through, and you can understand the stories even if not the sermons supposedly designed to explain or "preach on" them. Thus the inner city disciple occasionally hears of disciples being fishermen (Mk.1 16-20), being called provincial Galileans (Acts 2.7), unlearned and ignorant (Acts 4.13). Or they hear of people asking in astonishment where Jesus got his teachings from (Mk 6.2), and wonder what happened to that tradition in the contemporary educated Church.

Or the urban disciple hears the frequent condemnations of his disciples uttered by Jesus (Mk. 8 17b-18 etc), and wonders why it was alright to be seriously eccentric in your faith then, but not now. Or he/she hears about a poor widow giving a tiny coin, proclaimed as having given more than some other wealthy donors (Mk 12. 41-44), and wonders why the Church today does well among the rich but pretty badly among the poor. Or she hears the story about the baby wrapped in swaddling clothes, lying in a manger (Lk 2.12), and wonders why single mothers out on the streets are not inside the churches. Or he hears that the temple offerings of Jesus' parents were those of the poorest (Lk 2.24) and wonders why the pigeon-keepers seem so unwelcome now.

Or, in Church, the inner city or housing estate Christian wonders why when a church leader comes, they are spoken to patronisingly, if the leader has to be as the servant (Mk 10. 42-45). Or why when the circuit or deanery is on parade, the small churches are introduced with a condescending smile, if "Where two are three are gathered together, there is the Lord" (Mt 18.20). Or why, when the churches tell their stories, the tales of rich or successful churches are told, but not those of poor or unsuccessful ones, if this is a community in which "the last shall be first and the first last". (Mk 9. 35).

From these experiences and many more like them, the inner city or housing estate Christian builds up a firm suspicion, based on repeated experiences of listening and participating, that, whatever this story was about in the first place, it has got perverted by being adapted to the lifestyles, mindsets and vested interests of professional clergy, middle class Christians, and a generally status quo view of society, largely indistinguishable from that of everyone else in the surrounding society.

2. A Return to the Gospel

So, the inner city and housing estate Christians feel more and more alienated from the rest of the church, and from other Christians.

In this situation, they have to keep going back to the Gospel stories, to see if they had heard them properly after all!

And, the more the Christian in the poor church hears of the story, the deeper she becomes convinced that the story "fits" the poor church situation. According to Mark, Jesus abandoned the synagogue and worked from working class houses and households, being confined to one particular lower class area, notably Capernaum (1.29; 2.1, 15; 3.20; 5.38; 9.33). When he went to other areas he still ministered in houses and households (7.17, 24; 9.28; 10.10; 14.3). Jesus was located in a "working class" fishermen's location (1.16-20), lived in an ordinary village house with an easily removable roof (2.1-4), told stories of crops and farmers (4. 1-38),and got into trouble with the authorities for perceived illegal practices (2. 16-20).

All this feels very much like the life of an inner city area, or a housing estate. The so-called "pastoral" or "countryside" or "rural" feel of the stories is not the barrier that middle class people seem to perceive it to be. Here is Jesus, a small town local hero, with working people around him, walking and acting and speaking to and about local people and places. The context could be anywhere where someone is street-wise, knows the local scene, loves the local folk, and retells local down-to-earth stories which confirm the attitudes and preconceptions of the culture. It is not the geographical context but the social and cultural context that gives sense to it all, and places the hero in the easily comprehensible role of local community spokesperson, catalyst and natural leader.

If this is even remotely correct, there is an understandable resistance from the bottom to the top-downwards version of Christianity peddled still by the denominational and academic spokespeople and scholars. The unavoidable suspicion is that they have taken over happenings, people and stories with which they are in fundamental opposition, or at least existential non-sympathy, and used them for their own devices.

Inevitably, readers in a poor church or a poor area, reading the typical commentary, feel ill at ease. First, we do not experience things the same way as the narrative seems to be understood by the contemporary exegete!. Second, we do not live in the same "world" as the writer. Third, we are experiencing things that seem important that are not noticed, so we wonder if the writer has ignored important pieces of data. Fourth, we can produce a better understanding of Scripture itself when we incorporate our own viewpoint.

These four points are precisely the points in Segundo's "hermeneutics of suspicion" (2). Such a hermeneutic has been developed in feminist interpretation. In the words of Elizabeth Schussler Fiorenza:

"A feminist hermeneutic of suspicion questions the underlying presuppositions, androcentric models and inarticulated interests of contemporary biblical interpretation." (3)

All writers bring their own presuppositions, assumptions and hidden agendas with them, which "creates the linguistic invisibility and marginality of women, characterises them in stereotypical roles and images, and trivialises their contributions." (4)

Precisely this is what the urban Christians experience at the hands of the typical middle class Christian or exegete. They have become invisible and marginalised, they are characterised in stereotypical roles and images, and their contributions are trivialised.

This kind of negative feeling does not take away the Gospel from them. They still feel quite sure that the Gospel stories are about people like themselves, and situations like theirs. As a lay colleague and preacher in the Sheffield Inner City Ecumenical Mission put it:

"When I hear Jesus , as I do through the Gospel, then it seems to me that he's very much talking not only to the people of the inner city, but about the people of the inner city. That means he's speaking to the other areas of the city about those who we've learned to say are the ones who are at the bottom." (5)

This experience is echoed by many in the poorer churches and poorer areas. Once they are freed to respond to the stories themselves, they discover Jesus and a Gospel which is "for them" and even more "from them".

So the urban disciples are beginning to tell their own stories which seem to be like the Gospel stories. They sit down with the Gospel story in one ear and the stories from the street in the other.

3. Good News in Britain

So, UTU began to publish a "People's Bible Studies" series. A recent volume in this series, Good News in Britain (6) is a first attempt to try to put some of this down. It originated in 1992 when several inner city and housing estate churches were studying the excellent Christian Aid/CAFOD Lent booklet, Good News. They appreciated the down-to-earth stories coming from poor people and marginalised people in South America. They appreciated the way the Gospel stories were used to confirm or extend or critique the stories. They appreciated the prayers coming from poor people in poor churches. But then they said: "We have things like this taking place here also. Why are the stories and signs of the Gospel in Britain not told and celebrated and prayed for?"

Good News in Britain tries to celebrate the way that people in poor churches, housing estates and inner cities experience the Gospel stories as their own stories. (7)

Thus, Jesus' declaration of the Kingdom's presence in Mk 1.15 and his statement concerning his own mission in Lk 4. 16-20 raise some questions, like "for whom is the message "good news"?" The message is plainly good news for those who want to "change themselves completely" (metanoia, Mk 1.15), to the poor, the captives, the blind, and the oppressed. (Lk 4.18). So the question arises, whose good news happenings get to be regarded as Christian gospel happenings today? A black community worker said," Well, it's like a situation where we suddenly had the chance to employ a black community worker, and all the white clergy found every reason not to do it, and someone exclaimed "Let's not shut doors before we've even opened them". An inner city worker said she could only keep faith in God by denying most of the things people attributed to God. She ended up praying (with an Iona prayer book) "Help me to let go of the God I no longer believe in, and take hold of the God who believes in me". In each case, there is a struggle as to what is Good News, as to what belongs to the Christian Gospel.

The witness from the cities is clear: We have things like the Gospel stories happening now. "Get up and Walk" in Mk 2. 1-12 asks whether "starting with Confession" is good news for the inner city deprived, and whether a woman who prays with her prostitute neighbours is forgiving their sins or keeping them sinning. "The Widow's Mite" in Mk. 12. 41-44 is heard as applauding a little girl who empties her purse of coppers, the Muslims who celebrate by giving away money, and a black Pentecostal woman who gives away all her money and says "God will provide". "Leaving self behind" in Mk 8. 31-38 is heard to be about a research student "getting out of science", about a teacher losing her promotion by going to Africa, about a trader buying a shop in a poor area. Jesus going into the city on a donkey in Mk. 11 1-10 is seen as being about a community worker upsetting Church expectations, or about a woman whose husband gets Alzheimer's disease gaining a new ministry with others who suffer.

I believe that there is a rediscovery of the Gospel as good news for the poor going on in our midst. At least, a few people who thought they didn't belong in it at all are finding that, after all, their first suspicions were right -

that Jesus was, despite his interpreters, a friend of publicans and sinners, and someone whom the common people heard gladly. (Mk 12.37).

4. Critique from the Bottom

The inner cities and housing estates often feel themselves to be alienated from sources of power and influence, and to be the victims of authorities, decisions and enforcement officers from the city centre. As such groups read or hear the Gospel, they begin to feel a kinship with Jesus and his friends. The contemporary social, political and economic force of the practice of Jesus encourages those at the bottom to identify their oppressors and enter into a radical critique of the structures and people in power in society from the point of view of those at the bottom.

Jesus is also discovered to engage in a radical critique of the privileged, from the point of view of the underprivileged. Mark's Gospel is clear. The requirements of segregated table fellowship (2. 16-20) are only capable of being obeyed by the rich and those living in one-faith areas. The demands for fasting (2. 18-22) are only for those in the settled predictable eating habits of the middle class status quo, not for those grubbing for bits of food on the edges of someone else's cornfields. The demand for Sabbath observance or regarding the holiness of dedicated bread (2. 23-28) is excellent, but not for those who have no bread and not for those who have no recognised humanity. Keeping Sabbath in the synagogue is excellent, but getting your withered arm healed is even better (3. 1-6). Washing before meals (7. 1-23) is a useful ritual, but not if it has become an excuse for totally ignoring the commandment of God, which relates to inner evils such as covetousness and oppressing others (7. 21-22).

Such things reveal the well-known bias of legal systems in favour of the established order of society, represented by the rich and powerful, and against the natural justice of human expectations, based on the equality of all people before God and the law. So much is well known. But the personal application of it is particularly painful for those at the bottom. The Pharisees in Jesus' day represent the attempt to apply laws and customs which were originally designed to secure justice for all. But they had become in Jesus' day the means whereby those with the money to secure freedom of choice could remain righteous. The Pharisaic experts end up oppressing the people. They invent regulations whereby the elderly can be ignored and robbed (7. 9-13). They allow a man to "put away" his wife, leaving the woman bereft of livelihood (10. 1-9), thus denying the sacred reciprocity of two becoming one (10. 6-9). Such things are often what the rich and powerful do to the poor and weak.

People who live today in multi-faith and multi-cultural areas cannot afford segregated tables, or fasting, or Sunday observance, or meal rituals. But they usually stand beside their old folk. And they often stand beside their partners, even whey they would prefer them gone. Like the nuclear community of the Kingdom of God which Jesus set up in his disciple group, the urban disciple community today represents perhaps a new humanity, a new "Son of Man", free of race and class and economic and cultural distinction, perhaps because, being nearer the bottom, they know what the basics of human existence are, and what it is that moulds and even secures human beings in mutuality and survival and in the hope of significance - very like the simple basic rules and common life of Jesus and his disciples.

When we in the inner city study Jesus' practice, we are surprised that anyone could ever have thought that he was a friend of the middle class. Even his own contemporaries get recorded for their clearly embarrassing accusation that he is a "friend of publicans and sinners" (Matthew 11.19 cf Mk 2.16). This Jesus is a national health doctor who observes the rule that if your need is seen first, you get first treatment, regardless of who in authority has to wait (Mark 5. 21-43). This Jesus is easily persuaded against his principles or better judgement, when a mother's child is in need (7. 24-37). This Jesus prefers the child - always the idol of the poor, for whom nothing is ever good enough - to the power-seeking adult (9. 33-37). This Jesus prefers that people get healed and whole, regardless of who does it (7. 38-42). This Jesus prefers the poor to get help, rather than that all the old laws be obeyed (10. 17-22). This Jesus reckons the chances of the non-poor entering the Kingdom to be about as good as that of a camel getting through a needle's eye (10. 23-31). This Jesus can be followed by anyone who throws away all else to receive sight and throws away the crutches of their old existence (10. 46-52).

So our Man goes "on to the end" as "our God and our Friend", as Stainer's Crucifixion magnificently has it. The donkey he sits on suits him. He's not going anywhere fast, and he always compares himself downwards, not upwards (11. 2-7). He is the upstart pretender from the outback, entering the city of the powers. The powers see him as a rebel and a bandit - the two are allied. He is arrested as a bandit (14. 48), he is rejected for another bandit (15.7), he is crucified with two bandits (15.27).To the Jewish and Roman authorities Jesus appears as a rebel, a social bandit, a revolutionary, even though in fact he advocated no such policies.

The urban disciple sees in Jesus' entry into Jerusalem, his overturning the temple money tables, his cursing of the fig tree, his damning of the great temple buildings, his contempt for the temple authorities, a premonition of the bedraggled groups of inner city and housing estate people wending their way down to the Town Hall and trying to see the City authorities, but being ultimately tried and excluded by the contemporary wielders of social and economic power.

A recapitulation of the Jesus story is daily on our streets. He said he was Son of Man, and, by God, he has released into human history a succession of pathetic and heroic Don Quixotes, who march daily against the windmills of power, with clodhopping feet and dogged persistence, futilely to lay before the powers-that-be the hopes and claims for a fair and generous humanity, an open and free wholeness for all.

5. A New Hearing for the Gospel

In Sheffield now, I live over the hill from Meadowhall - the greatest shopping precinct in England, or Europe, or the galaxy? You can walk down the hill from Pitsmoor, Grimesthorpe or Wincobank (my places) to get to Meadowhall. You can walk the miles of Meadowhall's heated walkways, with bright lights and piped music, and pretend that you belong to the new generations with cars who come from miles around. But if you want to buy anything, you walk or bus to the still just-surviving Sheaf and Castle Markets, and buy cheap vegetables, meat and fish or (on Mondays) pick up second-hand oddments at the Flea market, or (on Wednesdays) second-hand clothes at the Rag Market. Or, for better quality clothing, you go a bit further to the West of the city, where their luxury cast-offs are cheap in the charity shops.

As a student of the Gospels, and of Mark in particular, and as a disciple of Jesus, I cannot but reflect on all this in the light of the archetypal story of Jesus. Jesus grew up in Nazareth, amidst the multi-cultural, multi-faith, anti-establishment Galilean culture, with its unemployed people in the market place, its beggars on the streets, its women holding the society together, its street-corner politics and its street-wise philosophers and, of course, its occupying Roman army. But over the hill, only five miles away, in Jesus's day the carpenters and builders and the servicing women came in from all the neighbouring towns and villages to build a great new Roman city, the city of Sepphoris.

Nowhere in the Gospels is there even a hint of Sepphoris' existence - much less that Jesus ever went there. But it would have been odd if the growing lad had never wandered down into the glittering lights of the new city on his doorstep - if he had not left the streets of Pitsmoor or Grimesthorpe or Wincobank to participate even if only as a spectator in the bright lights of Meadowhall.

There is a new hearing for the Gospel on our streets as the story of Jesus in his time strikes home in the lives of urban people today. Interestingly three bits of the contemporary theological scene have come to encourage us.

1. There has been in Biblical studies a concentration on the geographical, historical, social, cultural and political factors surrounding the work of Jesus and the earliest Jesus movements - for there were several, not least the long-observed Galilee-Jerusalem contrast. The work of Norman Gottwald, or scholars like Richard Horsley, John Dominic Crossan, Ched Myers and others (8) has raised the profile of a Jesus who inescapably belonged to the number of popular people-based radical revolutionary leaders who, time and again, allied themselves to popular messianic hopes and sought in some way for the common people to overcome the intolerable oppression heaped upon them with almost equal force by Roman occupying armies and governors, high priestly aristocratic co-rulers, a self-seeking and rapacious Herodian house and the economic power of Sadduccees, all of which took local form in Galilee in terms of economic oppression by non-local absentee landlords.

In this context, the Pharisees, in their attempts to secure the people in obedience to the Law, although they themselves were usually not rich or powerful, played a role of compliance and piety, which merely supported the oppressive status quo. Jesus in this context allied himself against all the "powers that be". His conflicts with the Pharisees were because they alone of the groups had any grassroots contact with the ordinary people. Jesus' "solution", of course, differed from all the others, but his practice, teaching and policy can only be assessed as alternative ways of dealing with the same realities. (9)

2. Equally useful and productive has been a second development in contemporary Gospel studies. It is now generally agreed that our reading of the text from our own contexts has to be added to a whole variety of writers and readers in the earliest church from whom or for whom different Gospels were written. New Testament and contemporary biblical studies speak in

terms not only of the traditional disciplines of Literary, Form and Redaction Criticism, but also in terms of Narrative Criticism, studying the story of a Gospel as a whole, Reader-Response Criticism, asking how a Gospel's potential or actual readers could have influenced the writing, and Social Criticism, asking how one social class's story might be modified if writers or readers belonged to another. At the contemporary end, other perspectives of contemporary critics are added - those of Deconstruction, Feminism and Materialism. (10)

All this means that the location of the writer and the reader are decisive. A location is both of "blood" (family, race, gender, sexuality, psychology) and of "bread" (location, livelihood, dependencies, socio-economic reality) (11). The location of reader and writer determines what the writer writes and what the reader hears. So that the urban reader can rightly ask how others hear the reading they are hearing. Even in the New Testament itself, writers are influencing the story. Referring to the Jesus traditions which "speak overwhelmingly for his deliberate participation in social conflict", Norman Gottwald comments:

"These socially confrontational traditions are now enclosed in redactions primarily interested in interpreting Jesus theologically and in toning down the harshness of Jesus' sociopolitical critique of the Jewish and Roman authorities who stood at the pinnacle of his society. The general failure to pursue this discrepancy probably follows from the fact that redaction critics more nearly share the social class perspective of the Gospel redactors than they do the social class perspective of Jesus." (12)

3. The rise of Liberation Theology in Britain, finally, also supports this hearing. If the disciples at the bottom of British society begin very tentatively to feel that the Gospel could possible even be on their side, they are helped by the example, method and theologising of those in many lands, mainly outside Britain, who have developed distinctive indigenous forms of liberation theology. In my experience, many of those who live and work here, and some of the "incomers" who have joined us, describe their beliefs and commitments in liberation theology terms. (13)

At this stage, liberation theology in Britain is not a new closed system, but certainly is a new method based upon a variety of significant stances and commitments in British society today. The urban disciples of the Gospel are, I believe, the most significant of those stances and commitments.

Footnotes:

1. Cf. my essay "Mark's Gospel in the Inner City" in The Bible and the Politics of Exegesis, ed. D Jobling, PL Day, & GT Sheppard (Cleveland: Pilgrim Press 1991) pp 275-290

2. J L Segundo The Liberation of Theology, (Maryknoll: Orbis 1976), p9

3. Elizabeth Schussler Fiorenza, Bread not Stones, (Boston: Beacon Press, 1984) p.16

4. Op cit, p.17

5. Amy Richinson quoted in my, Discipleship in the 90's (Methodist Publishing House, 1990), p.14

6. John Vincent, Good News in Britain, (Urban Theology Unit, 1994)

7. For the following two paragraphs, cf. Good News in Britain, pp 6-19

8. Cf. Richard Horsley, with JS Hanson, Bandits, Prophets and Messiahs: Popular Movements in the Time of Jesus (San Francisco: Harper & Row, 1985); JD Crossan, The Historical Jesus: the Life of a Mediterranean Jewish Peasant (Edinburgh: T&J Clark, 1991); Jesus: A Revolutionary Biography (London: Harper & Collins 1995); Ched Myers, Binding the Strong Man: A Political Reading of Mark's Story of Jesus (Maryknoll NY: Orbis, 1988)

9. Cf. my Tawney lecture "Jesus as Politician", in John Smith and others, Reclaiming the Ground (London: Hodder & Stoughton, 1993), pp 67-90

10. On the various contemporary approaches to the Gospels, see the essays in Mark and Method: New Approaches in Biblical Studies, ed JC Anderson and SD Moore (Minneapolis: Fortress Press, 1992), and The Open Text: New Directions for Biblical Studies? ed Francis Watson (SCM Press, 1993)

11. See especially: Reading from this Place Vol 1. "Social Location and Biblical Interpretation in the United States", ed Fernando Segovia and Mary Ann Tolbert (Minneapolis: Fortress Press, 1995). The reference to "The facts of blood and bread" is from Adrienne Rich, quoted by Mary Ann Tolbert on page 331. Cf. my article, "The Challenges and Responsibilities of Contextual Theology", Reviews in Religion and Theology, February 1997, pp 7-13

12. Norman Gottwald, "Social Class as Hermeneutical Category", Journal of Biblical Literature, 112/1 1993, pp 3-22, p 17-18

13. John Vincent, Liberation Theology from the Inner City (Urban Theology Unit, 1992)

Laurie Green

GOSPEL FROM THE UNDERCLASS

As our work continues, we are becoming more aware of, and intrigued by, the existence of the so-called "underclass" in the Urban Priority Areas. The phenomenon was described to me recently by a woman who used the image of a boat as representing our society. Unfortunately some, the "underclass", had not proved able-bodied seafarers and had fallen overboard and were therefore presently unable to enjoy the benefits which those in the boat of society enjoyed. Working from this image of the situation it was clear to her just what our task should be - to let down as many ladders into the sea as possible in order to allow those poor unfortunates to clamber their way back into the boat of plenty. My response to her description was to ask whether it was not possible to conceive of a society that did not force people overboard in the first place.

Even the term "Underclass" itself seems an oppressive word, forcing us to think in terms of the marginalised, people scorned as things of lesser worth and value than those in the so-called "upper" classes. But the term has the advantage of focussing sharply and vulgarly the realities of oppression that are at work in our economy, our culture and even in the language we use to describe the phenomena of alienation. Let us look a more closely at the phenomenon of the so-called "underclass".

1. The Growth of a Class Structure

On looking at our present British society, we observe those who appear to hold the reins of power through inherited wealth, culture-control (which I

Laurie Green has been Bishop of Bradwell, Essex, since 1992. A UTU DMin graduate and now Honorary Lecturer, he has two current UTU booklets, God in the Inner City (1993) and Jesus and the Jubilee (1997).

now take to include political control), welfare-control, high income and private capital. On first sight our inclination would be to call them the masters of our society, but this would be to misunderstand its complexity and the power which a structure can develop over its originators.

Over against this small group stands the vast majority of men and women who sell their labour and expertise as they can. The system of rewards is largely determined by one's ability to play one's part in the maintenance and furtherance of the overall system, and there has therefore grown up within this majority a large army of middle classes whose task is to inculcate into the hearts and minds of all, a type of pseudo-rationality which maintains the status quo by arguing that the basic system of our society is moral, normal and just. This is "technological rationality", which is designed to convince us that the given system is natural and right so that any injustice we perceive must be due to our not operating the given system correctly, using the wrong social "technology". Any fault in the structure is seen as merely malfunction or lack of appropriate technique within this best of all possible social structures/systems. Any idea that the system itself could be irrational or immoral is disallowed. This way of thinking has received a major boost of late with the demise of eastern European state capitalism under the guise of Communism. So we hear repeated the simple myth formulation, "There Is No Alternative" - TINA. The inculcation of this "technological rationality" at a deep level in the psyches of society's members is of such overriding priority that those who are set aside to perform this controlling function have usually reaped handsome rewards of finance, security and status for so doing. Sometimes they are even allowed to own a little of the basic international capital itself.

So the Middle Classes find themselves differentiated from others in the labour pool by being given responsibility for the operation of the system of checks and balances that keep the system operative in relation to the advancement of capital. This differentiates them from what we might still call the "working class", who have only their labour to offer to those who operate the checks and balances. Above them all are the persons and institutions which own and govern capital - insofar as it can be governed, for Mammon had always a mind of its own.

But below the whole edifice has hung those who are not of present use to the system. Marxists have called this group the Lumpen Proletariat - those at the bottom, those "overboard" who never are able even to get a hand-hold on the boat in which the others ride. They remain without security unless it is offered them in welfare provision life-buoys thrown to them from the boat, life-buoys which are designed to keep them just afloat but are not designed to get them out of the water. Precisely, this is "the poverty trap".

During the peak period of mechanical industrial advance, the overall system required a massive work-force of manual (even brutish) producers of the given work schedule. This large workforce had to be physically centred around the raw materials of production and sources of power, and therefore were thrown together sufficiently to be able to organise themselves into Trades Unions. In order to keep control of such a large and uniteable work-force, it was expedient to maintain a vast surplus army of unemployed, should workers demand overmuch. In this respect at least the Lumpen Proletariat was seen to be performing some function. But now things have changed radically.

2. Why the Classes are now undergoing Change

Having served the needs of capital in order to provide the basis of its wealth the working class has more recently been asked to perform another function, but this has demanded a significant shift in its role in relation to capital. With the advent of increased computerisation and automation of production, the need for producers has given way to an increasing need for consumers. The cultural superstructure has therefore shifted rapidly to provide the acquisitive society that capital now requires. Change in male sexual role models epitomises this change. Advertising has, in a period of only twenty years, moved the working -class male population from being fascinated by machinery, solidarity and production into a much more effeminate mode of finding interest in fashion, perfume and consumerism. Feminism has also played its part in moving the male into this new role as subservient to the needs of the new Capitalism. This shift in role models offers to the needs of capital a more subdued, acquisitive and a less physically dangerous and less mechanically concerned working class. The means of production having shifted, it was necessary to effect this very significant change in human society.

Added to this shift from a mechanical to an electronic base in the means of production was the demolition of the industrial base of British society by between a quarter and a fifth in the early years of the Thatcher government. So with the gathering pace of the shift away from the sort of productive industry which requires a large manual work-force came also the reduction of the employing industries, resulting in the fearful shift towards unemployment on a very large scale.

Those in labour had always been able to look down on the Lumpen Proletariat as part of the reserve pool of labour, but long-term unemployment and deskilling led to vast numbers of the working classes joining the ranks of the Lumpen Proletariat. There was always a fluid relationship between the Proletariat and the Lumpen Proletariat but now this fluidity had grown to the proportions of a swelling river. This new group by virtue of an ironic "trickle down" of poverty, has grown and is now found overwhelmingly in the Urban Priority Areas and the rural pockets of deprivation as the new (or not-so-new?) "underclass". By many they are considered superfluous to society and unable to contribute anything to it.

People on this bottom rung of the ladder were considered redundant to the productive system and therefore unnecessary to its continuation. Labour was cheaper elsewhere, machines could be programmed to do the work, and a reserve pool of labour was no longer necessary to keep others under the threat of unemployment, since all in work began to see that threat looming in any case. Latterly, however, they also became redundant to capital's problem of over-supply. Were they to be able to consume in quantity, then they would remain useful at least as consumers. But since in order to do this they would have to be paid more than subsistence wages, the mainstream of society does not reckon that the benefit to themselves of offering higher welfare payments would be worth the outlay. So they become a "written-off-class", quiet and subdued by their marginalised status, the dictates of the dominant cultural controls and their own absorbing concern to survive the poverty traps designed to sap their energies.

A large body of Marxist opinion has assumed the Lumpen Proletariat to be of little use as a lever to change society for the better, for in their eyes they have never had the necessary economic power to force others from the seat of control. Even capitalists now agree that this "written-off" or "under-" class can be tolerated by society because it is really no threat to its security. The underclass is not dangerous because there is little or no opportunity for the building of solidarity or self-awareness within its ranks. Its members still serve however to remind the "haves" to hang on grimly to the status quo and to what they have, lest they slip and join the dispossessed. On the other hand the underclass does cost the system in welfare payments, and therefore their numbers and their need have to be minimised statistically in order that a reduced social security budget can be legitimised.

There is clearly a need for a thorough analysis and appreciation not only of the economic bases of this exploitation but also of the social structures of domination, inculcation and persuasion which keeps society in subjection to this oppressive condition. Social control in technological cultures can be

120

achieved often without recourse to the nevertheless ever-present institutions of physical coercion.

It is now possible to reach down and control groups and individuals at the psychic level, and the cultural superstructure performs this function. So it is that bureaucracy, arts, literature, church, school, commerce, welfare, family, TV, Trades Unions, and the multiplicity of similar institutional safety valves serve the status quo and control the imagination of humankind. Human beings are thus reduced to being the nuts and bolts of the machine they serve. Even the capitalists are dominated by the myths that have been designed to maintain the system that serves them. Witness the way in which even Nigel Lawson and Margaret Thatcher came to believe their own hype regarding the boom that they had falsely initiated before the 1987 election. It is not simply the "market" that they cannot buck, but their every move, love and imagination functions within the place determined by the cultural regime they help sustain - based upon the economic infrastructure of capital. As Marcuse put it, we have all become "One Dimensional".

3. The Arena of Struggle

What I want now to argue for is that there is a dynamic relationship in society between any economic infrastructure and the cultural superstructure which rests upon it. Although the superstructure may be conditioned by the economic infrastructural forces, nevertheless there is nothing to prevent culture from reacting upon that determining structure to change it. For into the battle for change come culture, art, aesthetics, literatures, education, the media, politics, religion - and even theology! Each can use its own system of key language and symbols in the struggle to unblinker society and divest the dominating idea-sets of their power, by calling into question their rationality and pointing to those whom those idea-sets serve. Most of us are aware nowadays of the importance and critical nature of these cultural control factors, but many remain unaware still of its responsive and dynamic nature. So for example, while Marcuse bids us understand the superstructure in somewhat rigid and unresponsive terms, Gramsci as we shall see, views the cultural superstructure as a battle-ground where opposing factions must engage to win control of hegemonic forces.

We find similar ideas in the New Testament. St John the Divine understood that the power which social structures of domination wield is largely dependent upon the perception which members of that society have of them. By refusing to acknowledge the authority of the Beast, by refusing to worship it or carry its mark, the Christian witnesses confronted its power to control the perceptions of the members of that society. (Rev. 13 & 14). St John thus demands that Christians look elsewhere for transcendence and not to the Emperors or Pax Romana.

St Paul casts his net even wider by taking old cosmological myths and depersonalising, demythologising and then remythologising them. So, the "Principalities and Powers", he maintains, do have their rightful and God-given place; there is room in God's Kingdom for structures and form. But Christ's refusal to bow to their determination to dominate gives us the correct pattern and praxis in the struggle, so that now those self-same structures can be made to serve the Transcendent and no longer try to obliterate it or claim it for themselves. (cf. Col .2 v9-15; Eph.1 v20-23).

John sees the struggle as resulting in an all-out war to bring the dominating forces into line. Paul, like John, acknowledges that this battle has been fought and won by Christ, and we now reap the fruits of that victory. Our perceptions are changed. We see ourselves as free servants no longer to the structural demand of Law and race, and yet still living with these things present, given to us as a means of preventing society degenerating into chaos (Rom. 3 v 21-31; 7 v1-13). With this awareness, Christians are now able to view these same cultural constraints more objectively and can use them or deny them as the Divine Transcendent demands.

It is interesting therefore to compare how the Italian Marxist, Gramsci, emphasised the importance of the power of the control structures of culture and ideology, or as he termed it, "civil society". It was this preponderant influence over society, this dominance, this "ideological hegemony" which became his abiding concern. The distinctive feature of Gramsci's contribution to the Marxists' debate was his realisation that the "civil society" was no static monolith but rather an arena of struggle and conflict, in which we had to engage. The structures and means of cultural control are of a dynamic nature, and there is no reason to suppose that they cannot be won over in the cause of justice and democracy. How this power is gained and how it is used became the keynote of his deliberations upon praxis.

It does not take much to recognise the parallels between Gramsci's call for constant critical refusal to accept the domination of the prevailing hegemonic ideologies and structures, and St John the Divine's stand against the invidious creeping evil of the structures of Emperor deification, and his introduction of Christian symbolism over against the hegemonic symbol of the Emperor cult. Gramsci's goal is that these hegemonic constructs be used in the just service of the oppressed. That is, they will have their place in his Utopia as means by which a mass socialist consciousness will be made to support a society of justice and sharing. The parallel in our Christian tradition might then be St Paul's understanding of the new just function which will be served by the Principalities and Powers once they have been divested of their falsehood and brought back into the proper role for which their creator intended them. (Cf. Colossians 2. v 14-15, assuming Paul as author).

Our task then is to use our theology, both theological words and theological actions, to hold up the dominant cultural ideologies of society to the scrutiny of the Kingdom of God criteria. Theology must call into question the dominant culture's understanding of the nature of power and its craving for it in every quarter. How then might this be done?

4. The Gospel Strategy

The Gospels provide for us a very strong account of the way in which Jesus undertook to locate, confront, question and do battle with the dominant cultural ideologies of his time and place. His methodology, as for example recorded for us in St Mark's Gospel, looks to be an ideal pattern for our own situation. Jesus first locates himself alongside those who are in the most marginalised of conditions in his society. From that perspective he uses the claims and criteria of the imminent Kingdom of God to critique that society from the underside. He therefore perceives what are the dominant factors operating in his contemporary society to keep God's poor oppressed.

The work of Ched Myers, Binding the Strong Man, helps us to locate the precise societal factors which Jesus focuses and confronts. First, Jesus targets the Purity Codes which were used by the Pharisees, Sadducees and Essenes to keep themselves potentially in control of society . The Codes thus abused offered society the security of a class structure dominated by the wealthy. The second dominant oppressing factor targeted by Jesus was the cultural myth of Debt and fault. In practical terms this related to the Priestly caste's control of land tax, "sin", tribute and tithe. The mind-set supported by this myth allowed the Priestly caste to exact from the poor and from the land, and at the same time gave them a direct line to the Roman authorities.

The first chapters of the Gospel give repeated examples of Jesus at war with the enslaving ideology of Purity: curing Peter's mother-in-law and then immediately eating at her hand; confronting in the holy Synagogue the Unclean Spirit; raising up the girl in puberty and the woman whose blood had indicated her impurity. Equally, the ideology of Debt is also confronted: Jesus releases the paralytic from all Debt, and wrests from the scribal and priestly caste their authority on earth to release from debt. He reclines with tax-gatherers and sinners because all are now equal before God, since in the Kingdom debts are forgiven. The Kingdom is inclusive. The Church today must locate itself alongside the poor and dispossessed in order to focus the dominating cultural myths of today. It must, like Jesus, move into action alongside the poor to explode those myths and parade them in order to see what their true worth is or is not.

It seems to me that it is only amongst the so-called Underclass that we are to find in today's society the equivalent locus for sensitive experience, opportunity for analysis and the comrades for symbolic/prophetic activity reminiscent of Jesus's Gospel method. The Underclass are to be compared in this dynamic with the "crowd" (Greek, Ochlos) of the New Testament, which is the omnipresent background of Jesus's ministry. The Ochlos is identified as consisting of sinners and social outcasts. Though differentiated from the disciples, they are accepted as part of Jesus's community. Unlike the disciples, they are never directly criticised, or given special instructions or conditions. They are alienated from the Jewish leadership. and thus largely supportive of Jesus in his struggle against that leadership. They are feared by the ruling class, which nevertheless in the end is able to manipulate them against Jesus. It is from their number that Jesus calls out the child and the man with the withered hand, and stands them in the middle of the throng. Thus he takes the lesser representatives of the oppressed, "the poorest of the poor", the "written off ones", the "underclass", and brings them to centre stage. The margins become the central focus of his praxis. The first become last and the last first. All this makes good sense in terms of Gospel theology. But it is also credible in socio-political terms, for it is from the perspective of the underclass that it is possible to perceive best the oppression of the cultural myths. And it is in this arena, as Gramsci explains, that the revolution must be framed in readiness for the right historical moment - in our terms, the Kairos.

5. Insights Into the Gospel

It is also important to appreciate that immersion amongst the underclass will help us understand the actions of Jesus as recorded for us in the Gospel. The oppressed are the continuing users of the Gospel language codes. We will thus find in the "underclass" a similar use of story as is found in the New Testament; a similar use of parabolic symbol, acted parable, apocalyptic hyperbole, cryptic political allusion and celebration in song. (Witness any good Rasta "Redemption Song".)

From within the underclass today we will, by paying strict attention to the stories of the People, be able "to hear the cry of our brother's blood crying out to God from the earth". We will listen with rapt attention. What we will hear I have tried to describe elsewhere, for example in my God in the Inner City. What we hear has to do with the need of the wider society to find again its ability to celebrate at the same time as acknowledging its sadness. It has to do with allowing the Spirit to pray through us, by which means we acknowledge God as Abba, Father, and so one another as brothers and sisters - from which flows all justice. It has to do with acknowledging our dependency, as not being self-made. It has to do with being aware of the dangers and joys of Power, acknowledging it as God's. It has to do with finding a new sense of place, so that we see ourselves as stewards of God's bountiful land, God's creation. It has to do with being hungry for fairness, from which can blossom a new world order. It has to do with helping us form a new theology of Grace over Works; and so on.

Faith in the City made the Church own up to the circumstances of the poor, but we still have to make the Church listen to what is heard from the perspective of the poor. It gave to the Church a vision of getting the poor out of poverty and quite rightly so, for poverty is sin against God. But it did not go on from there to investigate what vision lies beyond freedom from poverty. Most people in the East End of London seem to look at Salvation in terms of a safe mortgage in Brentwood or Basildon, and I can't honestly find much in Faith in the City which takes us beyond that hope. It seems then that we have not done enough to get under the skin of the cultural myths which continue to enslave even when poverty is relieved. (1) Theology can and must help here. But in order to do so, it must be a theology worked out from the perspective of a Gospel context. One such context is the perception of today's so-called "Underclass".

Books referred to:

Ched Myers, Binding the Strong Man (Orbis: 1988)
Laurie Green, God in the Inner City (Urban Theology Unit: 1993)

Footnote:

1.   See further my paper "The Jesus of the Inner City", in Ian K Duffield, ed. Urban Christ: Responses to John Vincent (UTU: 1997) pp 25-33

Chris Rowland

REFLECTION: THE CHALLENGE TO THEOLOGY

1. A Challenge to the Theologians

There is a danger in the process that I am about to embark on. Not only do I want to resist the temptation to put myself in some kind of Olympian position from which I can offer assessment on the theology of my colleagues, who have contributed to this volume, but I also want to avoid pretending that I am anyone other than an Oxford professor with a particular theological formation, albeit one that has been leavened by nearly two decades of contact with friends in the Urban Theology Unit. I can best do this by acknowledging that I, like them, have a context for my theology which shapes, empowers, and distorts what I do. I have a sense of responsibility to the academy, as well as a conviction that the academy is not the only, nor often the best, place for understanding the way of Jesus Christ. It is not just because of weakness or inertia that I have worked in Oxbridge for most of my academic life.

Yet, reading these pieces I feel uncomfortable, not only because of the sense of privilege (a response which can become debilitating and self-pitying), but also, and much more importantly, because I hear in the language used in them, echoes of the voices of Scripture - the experience of being an alien; the insignificant groups, dying in the world's terms, yet being a vehicle of gospel values, opening doors of the reign of God, not by

Chris Rowland is Dean Ireland's Professor of Holy Scripture at Oxford University. He is a regular visitor to UTU, where he is an Honorary Lecturer. Recent publications include the volume on Revelation in the Epworth Commentaries.

status; an eremitic life in an urban setting; value in the things given rather than what is taken; the presence of the beyond in the ordinary and mundane; dealing with a sense of loss; loving the poor rather than doing good to them (echoes of Wesley's pre- and post-conversion experience here, perhaps). These stories echo the Scriptures through the language which is sometimes used, although they may not always intend to do so.

A continuing challenge for myself, as a Christian theologian, is how to match the competing demands of the academy with those of the church, and in particular, those of the poor and marginalised. My thoughts often turn to a little story contained in The Martyr's Mirror, a collection of testimonies brought together by the Mennonites, to which I have often found myself returning when discussing the relationship of the academy to those without training in the language and particular expertise of academic theology, but whose experience of life has offered them an understanding of the ways of God which book-learning can never adequately offer. It offers an example of the contrasts between two types of learning. In Flanders, in the middle of the sixteenth century, a chandler called Jacob was detained for his Anabaptist activities and was subsequently questioned by a cleric. When the discussion turned to the Book of Revelation the scholar asked the chandler how it was possible he could understand about John's Apocalypse without any university education, when the likes of himself had attended the University of Louvain and still had not been able to fathom the mysteries of the Apocalypse. This provoked from the chandler the quotation of Matt. 11:25 - "I thank thee, Father, lord of heaven and earth, that you have revealed this to babes and hid it from the wise and intelligent." In response, the ecclesiastical interrogator mocked the claim that ordinary workers might understand God's revelation, whereas learned theologians who have studied might find themselves puzzled over the divine mysteries.

What is disconcerting about this story is the polarisation of the academically trained and the 'amateur' interpretation of Scripture. The implication is that academic endeavour may, in the end, prove to be superfluous, or even misleading, if it is not matched with that humility of experience and insight enjoyed by those who are marginal to society. This echoes a deep-rooted conviction from the very start of Christianity, that there may be occasions when the wisdom of God contrasts with and challenges the wisdom of the world, and all the learning in the world cannot facilitate an understanding of God and Scripture, whereas the wisdom of God is understood by those who, humanly speaking, one least expects to do so. Several passages in Matthew's gospel suggest the reversal of human expectations. At the conclusion of the eschatological discourse the heavenly son of man sits on a throne of glory (25.35ff.); but we soon learn that the son of man has been present in the midst of mundane circumstances of human need, in the persons of those who appear to be non-entities, the outcasts here and now in the midst of the earthly city and not only in heaven on the last day.

Jane Grinnoneau's experience points her to passages like Matt.18.1-6 where Jesus takes a child and instructs the disciples to identify with the child in order to be truly great. Just as fulfilling the needs of the hungry and the thirsty means doing it to the heavenly son of man, so receiving a child means receiving Jesus. The angels of the little ones stand in close proximity to the throne of glory and see God face to face; the destiny promised, according to Revelation, to those in the New Jerusalem. The angels are linked with those who, in worldly terms, are insignificant but who, from the divine perspective, carry a particular privilege. They have that insight referred to in the verse quoted by Jacob the chandler: "I thank you, Father, lord of heaven and earth, for hiding things from the learned and the wise, and revealing them to the simple" (Matt.11.25). Later in Matthew's narrative it is children, along with the lame and the blind, who greet the meek and lowly king in the Temple, whereas the hierarchy seek to persuade Jesus to rebuke the children (Matt.21.12-17). To place a child in the midst of the disciples is to challenge the assumption that the child has nothing of worth and can only be heeded when it has received another's wisdom. The ordering of things which characterises the adult world is not, after all, the embodiment of wisdom and may even be a perversion of it.

2. Liberation Theology and Conversion

I am aware that by juxtaposing the story from sixteenth century Europe with my writing of these reflections on the articles in this volume, I might appear to be a trained theologian and exegete writing patronisingly about the accounts contained therein. My point is, however, to seek to articulate one of the conundrums of liberation theology, that it offers a way of doing theology which involves an intellectual and theological conversion. There is another experience which complements, and may revolutionise, the learning of the academy. As the pioneers of liberation theology learnt, commitment to the poor and marginalised and the disorientation of life and the reflection on it which results, means embarking on another way of theology, not necessarily unrelated to the intellectual knowledge of a university, but a necessary environment for stimulating that intellectual activity which enables true theology to begin.

Liberation theology, therefore, is not a corpus of knowledge to be acquired from books, lectures, and seminars, but something to be learnt from life and its vicissitudes. These varied stories offer a reminder that theology is not just a matter of learning from books, but must be related to the experiences of life, particularly the circumstances of vulnerability and need. Liberation theologians speak of an 'epistemological break', which comes through commitment and discipleship, the reorientation of perspective which is the consequence of embarking on that journey of solidarity, an experience which cannot adequately be communicated except by participating in the process itself. Liberation theologians have reminded us of the importance of the dialectic between different disciplines, and, of recovering the hidden stories of the insignificant and misunderstood as we engage with Scripture's concern for the poor and the outsider.

In a theological education where there is a constructive dialogue between academic theology and the life of the Church, is there room for the contribution of an institution like Oxford? It is true that Oxford has, over the years, had a fruitful relationship with those training men and women for full-time ministry. The question is whether, in addition to sharing their expertise in the Christian tradition, it can support and enable that theologising which is going on, in different places, in very different modes, up and down the country. Theology in a university offers the possibility of benefit from other disciplines. There is a growing need for the different kinds of theologising to share their agendas. The Latin American experience suggests that the regular interaction of liberation theologians with 'ordinary readers' extends the scope of theological education far beyond the walls of university or seminary. I would like to echo Ernst Kasemann's remarks, "Were my work of no possible help to Dom Helder Camara in his troubles [at the time Kasemann was writing Camara was Archbishop of Recife and Olinda and a pioneer of liberation theology in Brazil], I would not remain a New Testament scholar."

Those of us involved in academic theology may have help in the complex task of interpreting texts, which are still a part of the fabric of communities in the contemporary world, not so much by offering ex cathedra judgements, but rather by offering questions as a resource to show up the sort of distortions which are all too easily masked by complacency. Whether we like it or not, texts are locuses of struggle, and all theology in one way or another, is contextual. Biblical texts in particular have always been tied up in a particular set of human struggles, because of their authoritative status.

The factors which exclude or render some voiceless in the interpretative process demand constant vigilance.

3. Oppressed People as Mediators of God

So, when I read these essays, I find myself challenged by their genre and wisdom. The honesty and transparency of what is shared, and the proximity of theology and personal testimony, contrasts with a tradition of academic discourse in which the autobiographical is rigorously eschewed. That eschewal might be appropriate at times, but whether it can be the norm for theology, I doubt. Yes, there can be a narcissistic tendency in which understanding of God is viewed solely through the eyes of one's own experience, which then becomes the criterion of theological rectitude. All of us, whether in the academy or UPA, need to be aware of that. There is a rich story of wisdom which in humility we need to listen to. That being said, however, experiences of being an alien, of poverty, of survival, of what John Vincent has called "the downward journey," of having one's eyes open to the persons of the poor and marginalised people by being one oneself, all echo those of the people of God in Scripture and down the centuries. What I read are accounts of oppressed people being the mediators of God. Eyes are opened to see the gospel in situations which, to outsiders, seem unlikely places to find God.

In response, the academic exegetes can respond in several ways. Firstly, they can point out that the text does not say what it is supposed to suggest. Secondly, as a result of the enormous amount of industry devoted to the reconstruction of the original setting and purpose, they can note the discrepancy between that reconstruction and contemporary attempts at appropriation. Thirdly, they can question the propriety of bridging the gap between ancient text and modern context.

All these strategies are at work in modern suspicion of actualisation: the application of Scripture to the modern world. The 'ordinary reader' is inevitably dependent on translation, a task sustained by historical and comparative linguistic study; there is no access to Scripture without resort to Greek, Hebrew, and Aramaic. There may be some force in some of the criticisms but, at the end of the day, there may be an understanding of Scripture open to those in situations of marginalisation and vulnerability which is either closed off to, or remote from, the situation of the intellectual enterprise of the modern academy. Radicals like Gerrard Winstanley wrote of God enabling ordinary folk having understanding by "testimony or proof of such things to be true by experimental discoveries," so that those who "could never read a letter in the book, might throw off the glove to all humane learning in the world, and declare the deceit of it."

This means that the learned should not put themselves in a position of being adjudicators of the text's meaning, but become participants in a common interpretative enterprise, in which they do not presume to hand down what the text means for consumption by 'ordinary readers.' They will have things to say, information to impart, and insight to complement what is on offer. But, in order to avoid a 'relay version' of the interpretative enterprise, in which expertise is handed down in suitably accessible forms, the interpretative practice of the academy has to be geared towards facilitating the enterprise and offering parameters within which the search for understanding and exploration of the Scriptures can take place.

There will be those who come to these texts convinced that they cannot understand them, and seeing no way in which they could possibly 'speak' to them. What is needed, in addition, therefore are ways of enabling the 'experimental discoveries' to take place. That is not the situation contemplated in the essays in this volume where such discoveries have emerged in the searing experiences of life. But it is now a pressing need among disciples everywhere.

LETTERS

RESPONSE TO LIBERATION THEOLOGY UK

It was a real delight to read such a stimulating collection of essays. So some thoughts in response:

I do agree with those who suggest that you cannot just lift Liberation Theology out of Latin America and implant it in the UK. The way life and faith, reality and the tradition work together is entirely different. I am not even too sure how far it can be related to poverty in the UK. Sure there are people who are marginalised and excluded, but relatively, Britain is a wealthy country - so maybe here liberation is from wealth, liberation from affluence, liberation from consumption, so as to create alternative economics, alternative work, alternative lifestyles. (cf the DIY culture of the road protesters and radical environmental movements).

Middle classness. This is certainly something that is, perhaps, especially British - is it the focal point of liberation theology in the UK? A liberated middle class have the power and the skills to develop alternatives. Alternative communities, LETS schemes, road protests, and radical environmental movements, all draw their vitality from the middle classes. Many of the tree-dwellers in the roads protests over recent years are well educated and articulate people, with all the skills necessary to "take one" government and business interests. Are there glimpses here of the kind of revolt against Constantinian established Christianity that led people - was it the middle classes? - into the desert to found new alternative communities of voluntary poverty and simplicity - the beginning of the monastic movement?

Chris Wiltsher's essay on the characteristics of the working class and lower middle class was to the point. His description of the "prejudiced, even' bigoted, blinkered, narrow-minded and self-centred with no interest in anything outside of an unhealthy lifestyle, sport and hearing about the latest sex sensation" is a cartoon of Ilkeston. Someone once said to me that the problem with Ilkeston is that is has no middle-class (nothing to liberate it??). I came here to liberate myself from the greed, fear and aggression of London, and have gradually come to discover that people here keep their noses hard to the grind stone to acquire all the things that I tried to escape from! It is the culture of consumerism that unites Britain, and nobody wants to be liberated from it,. So what do you do with liberation theology in a culture where people love their chains? Here people have neither the time or the interest to pursue the kind of wider "solidarity" type campaigns that Chris speaks of - it is an activists graveyard! Some short term interest when it is convenient, but the primary campaign is to have what everybody else has and to keep the consumer bandwagon rolling. Liberate that!

So I am not sure that in Britain we can talk about a "church of the poor", especially if the aim of this church of the poor is to make the poor rich and oil the wheels of the free market consumerist roller coaster.

What we might be able to talk about is a church of the alternative - a church that explores new values, new economics, new lifestyles, that is latently subversive in relation to the cultural status quo. Andrew Bradstock steers towards this in his essay especially in his section on a "Restated Liberation Theology", where he quotes Pixley on the need to resist the twentieth century "pax romana". Both the poor and the rich are locked into the consumerist treadmill, and the church of the alternative will draw across a wide spectrum.

Everyone wants a share of the cake, but what happens if you don't like cake - or want to bake a different one?

So thanks once again for a very stimulating and thought-provoking book.

Lyn Atterbury
Ilkeston

RESPONSE TO ANDREW BRADSTOCK

I am sympathetic to most of Andrew Bradstock's clear and thoughtful contribution on "Liberation Theology after the Failure of Revolution". I have, however, two reservations. Both spring from what I think is an overly pessimistic reaction to recent events. We should not allow the impressions of a decade to become the truth of a century.

First, I am loth to accept the view that the perceived failure of Marxism means socialism as a paradigm is lost to us. We should not forget that, for all its destructive excesses, the kind of Marxism practised in the Soviet Union, China, Cuba etc, did bring literacy, rudimentary health care and housing to millions of people - many of whom seem not to regret the disappearance of the socio-political system which guaranteed these amenities. Nor should we let the triumphalist account of Fukayama go unchallenged: his thesis about the end of history implies that contemporary liberal democratic societies adequately satisfy the basic human desire for equal recognition. Clearly they do not. Only a radical egalitarianism can ensure the full recognition of all - which must entail some form of socialism.

Second, while not rejecting the concentralism on small-scale projects, I do not think we should lose sight of the global perspective. For the "sectors" are linked and "community" in one is difficult without community in all.

Moreover, from one point of view, the collapse of communism brings Russia back into the course of history as outline by Marx - socialism is only possible following capitalism. If capitalism is triumphant world-wide, then on this (rather optimistic) view this sets the scene for socialism which only now can really become an agendum. To advocate new politics of community which somehow transcends left and right is to neglect the immense and varied riches of the socialist tradition. And if it is the private manipulation of major economic resources that is destroying community, then their common ownership/control is the only answer.

David McLellan
Canterbury University

LETTERS are welcome. Please send to the Editors, c/o Urban Theology Unit, 210 Abbeyfield Road, Sheffield S4 7AZ

CHRONICLE

THE INSTITUTE FOR BRITISH LIBERATION THEOLOGY

The annual Institute for British Liberation Theology met at the UTU in Sheffield for three days Tuesday-Thursday, 16-18 July 1996 and 22-24 July 1997. Several of the papers presented are in the present volume, or will be in the 1999 volume, Urban Spirituality. The Institute is open to everyone interested. Participants contribute a small charge, and arrange their own accommodation or pay for rooms at UTU. Please write with offers of contributions for the next Institutes, which will be Tuesday-Thursday, 21-23 July 1998 and Tuesday-Thursday, 20-22 July 1999.

Enquiries to: Rev Dr John Vincent
178 Abbeyfield Road, Sheffield S4 7AZ

At the July 1997 Institute at UTU, it was agreed to seek to arrange Regional Day or Weekend occasions in addition to the annual July event in Sheffield. Ms Bridget Rees and Dr John Vincent are now joint co-ordinators for the Institute. Please address enquiries to John or to:

Ms Bridget Rees
Community of the Resurrection, Mirfield, Yorks

THE BRITISH LIBERATION THEOLOGY
CONSULTATION AND CELEBRATION

The British Liberation Theology Consultation and Celebration is a bi-annual event held at Wistaton Hall, near Crewe. It is a sharing and supportive fellowship for people working in liberation theology style projects and ministries. The fifth Consultation and Celebration will take place on Friday-Sunday, 17-19 October 1997, then in October 1999. Enquiries to the joint Co-ordinators:

Mr Mike Simpson and Mrs Jean Sharples
c/o 16 Wellington Road, Nantwich CW5 7BH

Mike and Jean have written an account of the Consultations and Celebrations, which will be included in Liberation Spirituality.

THE INSTITUTE FOR BRITISH BLACK THEOLOGY

The Institute for British Black Theology is an annual meeting of workers and writers of British Black and Asian Theologies. Contributions are invited, which may become part of a proposed Journal. The Institute takes place at UTU in Sheffield. Future dates are Friday-Sunday, 3-5 July 1998, and in July of subsequent years. Enquiries to the Chair:

Rev Inderjit Bhogal
210 Abbeyfield Road, Sheffield S4 7AZ

DOCTORAL PROGRAMME IN
CONTEXTUAL, URBAN AND LIBERATION THEOLOGIES

An MPhil/PhD course in Contextual, Urban and Liberation Theologies, with Dr John Vincent as joint Supervisor, is accredited by the Biblical Studies Department of Sheffield University, using the Urban Theology Unit as base. Groups of candidates meet for 3-day periods quarterly in Sheffield over the first two years of the part-time course. Enquiries to:

Dr John Vincent
178 Abbeyfield Road, Sheffield S4 7AY

LIBERATION THEOLOGY UK

Reviews and Notices of our first volume were in many periodicals.

Notice should be made here especially of Gareth Jones' 7-page "Interview" with John Vincent, published in Reviews of Religion and Theology, August 1996.

URBAN CHRIST
Responses to John Vincent
Edited by IAN K DUFFIELD

URBAN CHRIST puts together a selection of pieces on Christianity as John Vincent lives and teaches it, with responses and critiques from friends and fellow workers. The sequence of studies begins in the challenge of discipleship (Elizabeth Mitchell), and subjecting theology to the practical test of what actually works (Ian Duffield). It then holds up a determinative figure of a radical Jesus, friend of the poor (Laurie Green), a thrust which puts it squarely with liberation theology and contemporary gospel study (Chris Rowland). It invites the Story Reader to become the Story Maker (Andrew Davey), to create a whole Dynamic life-scheme on the basis of it (Robin Pagan), to create politics out of it (Alan Billings0, and to work at present embodiments for Church and Mission (Colin Marchant).   £6.00

NEW CITY SPECIAL No. 12

JESUS AND THE JUBILEE
The Kingdom of God and our New Millenium
by LAURIE GREEN, Bishop of Bradwell   £1.50

A Reprint to meet continuing demand

HYMNS OF THE CITY
Edited by JOHN J VINCENT
New City Special No. 6   £1.00

A Basic Document for City Concerns

THE CITIES
THE METHODIST REPORT TO THE CHURCHES AND THE NATION
Published by NCH Action for Children. Available from UTU.
£10.00

Please add postage: 40p plus 15p per £1 over £1.00 order.
Send cheques payable to Urban Theology Unit to,
UTU, 210 Abbeyfield Road, Sheffield, S4 7AZ